BearFoot
A Northbounder
E-mails from the Appalachian Trail

PATRICK PITTARD

Illustrations by Lisa Chalmers

WILL
PUBLISHING, L.L.C.

BEARFOOT, A NORTHBOUNDER
E-mails from the Appalachian Trail

By Patrick Pittard

First Edition—2005

Published By
Will Publishing, L.L.C.
1029 22nd Street South
Birmingham, AL 35205

ISBN 0-9668486-2-4
Library of Congress Control Number 2005924618

Artwork by Lisa Chalmers
Book and Cover Design by Brooks Graphic Design

Printed in Canada

Dedicated to
DANA

ACKNOWLEDGEMENTS

Most importantly Tracy Jones Keiser. She was the hands to my thoughts, and has been for so long. She has retyped this manuscript as often as I hiked miles. To my many proofreaders, but particularly Tom Bailey, Jayne McAlister, and Gayle Nemeroff. To my kids, who kept pushing me to finish both the trail and the book—Leigh, Cole, and Brett. To Mary Gantt, my publisher, who can do anything. To Teresa Brooks, who can make chicken salad out of chicken droppings. For my family, who smiled and nodded when I said I was going to hike the AT, but celebrated at the finish—Buddy, Jo, Gerrie, David, Darcey, Stace, A.G., Granddaddy, and Nonnie.

There were friends on the trail. Pipe Wrench, who became my lifelong friend. Stone, I hope you are happy. April, Jeff, Sly, Wanderer, Birdnut, Highwater, Giggles, Cash, Dragonfly, Poet, and so many more.

There were those just off the trail who were there when it mattered. The deacon who picked me up and took me to the hospital in Erwin. Bob in Rangeley. My driver in New Hampshire who took me to the airplane. The Mitchells at 4-Pines. Jensine at Rainbow Springs. Brian and Kim at Penn-Mar. Carol and Jeff at Erwin. Lois and Earl at the Dutch House. The B&B owners who let me in when they shouldn't have. Folks who picked me up hitchhiking. George and Jane Benson for saving me at Hanover. David and Nancy for the break I needed.

Thank you all.

AN APOLOGY TO THE PURISTS

There are a bunch of Purists who hike. They are anal. They are factoids. They should have their Sharpie out when they read this book. They will have a ball identifying factual errors like, "He said that road north of Andover is East Road. Wrong! It's East B Road!" I have one comment to them. Eat me. Oops, two words. You're the guys who interrupt a terrific conversation to correct someone because he had a mileage sign off by one-tenth of a mile. Jesus! Get a life.

Just so you know I am pretty sure about all the facts in this book, but much of this was done writing in the dark, often on wet paper, sometimes I didn't write for a week, and then tried to catch up as best I remembered. Some of the facts here are hear-say. Sometimes to an AT thru-hiker reading this, it will seem I was a Southbounder, not a Northbounder. That is because I slacked-packed (explained later) as much as I could. Often I remembered something days, even weeks, later. I would write it down out of sync. I present it to you like I wrote it on the trail. If it seems to you I am having flashbacks, I am. If I came upon a group of hikers who were intersecting with me on another trail, and they said they were coming from Tyringham, I believed them. I did not confirm their story for purposes of this book. They could be coming from Ludiwizzee for all I cared. This is not a how-to book. You are an absolute fool if you take off from Springer using this as your trail guide. This is a why-to, not how-to.

I think Purists are the way they are because they never had an original thought. So their life is facts not vision. I put up with them on the trail because they couldn't help themselves. (And I have to admit, because they usually knew what they were talking about.)

So Purists I apologize. If the coffee is not free in Hot Springs, I apologize in advance. But please don't e-mail with that fact. Because, you know—I don't give a shit.

—Bearfoot

PUBLISHER'S NOTE

When you first meet Pat Pittard, it's obvious he is a successful businessman—educated, attractive, well read, and well traveled. This man—completely confident, perhaps even a bit aloof—did not appear to be someone interested in the deprivation of luxuries.

Yet, here he is with his personal story of hiking the Appalachian Trail–a grueling six-month journey of over 2,000 miles and his first hike *ever*—and I have to wonder *why?*

BEARFOOT, A NORTHBOUNDER answers the question. Not on one page or in one paragraph, but it is there.

Not being an outdoors enthusiast (my idea of roughing it means the Hilton), I did not expect to be so engaged by this story. A compilation of e-mails Pat sent from the trail, *Bearfoot, A Northbounder* took me into the breathtaking wilderness of eastern North America to experience everything he felt: the pain of a body pushed to its limits by hard terrain and punishing weather, the loneliness of separation from family and friends, the overwhelming awe of nature's astonishing power and beauty.

It was a little frightening at times. I smiled, cried, and even laughed out loud. I am so glad I made this trip. You will be too.

I discovered there is much more to Pat Pittard than meets the eye. He is compassionate and caring. He loves and appreciates his wife, family, and friends. He is strong and determined in a quiet, purposeful way. He is very much aware of himself and those around him. He loves history. He cares about animals. He gives back to the world. He is a southern gentleman. He is humbled by nature and true kindness. After reading his story, you will come to know this man and hopefully, know yourself better. And you will also know *why*...

Will Publishing is proud that we were allowed to help tell Pat's story.

MARY C. GANTT
Will Publishing, L.L.C.

"BEARFOOT, A NORTHBOUNDER starts as a story of a non-hiker CEO on an adventure. The first section is interesting in a comfortable way. But as the miles pile up, the adventurer starts to change as does his writing. It then becomes a must-read. Nothing important can be on your calendar as you approach this point in the book, because you won't put it down. This is not a go-there-next travel journal. As Bearfoot seeks solitude, his journey, that becomes your journey, is all about the wonder of people often at their best. Enjoy."

—*The Cherokee Rose*

FOREWORD

by **Pipe Wrench**

BEARFOOT, A NORTHBOUNDER is a tale of the modern American myth where "it is the individual that predominates the story, and it is for the sake of the individual that the hero seeks an adventure, fraught with uncertainty and the dragons of the soul." With the basic necessities of life covered, we naturally turn our eye inward and search for experiences which will broaden and deepen our understanding of who we are. By comprehending ourselves, we make sense of the world. Too often we think of myths as only epoch stories where the village is the object of the hero's actions, and the individual is simply the facilitator. Now we have a new tradition, and it is being played out in great numbers. Each spring, several thousand people set out into the world of uncertainty by attempting to thru-hike the Appalachian Trail (AT). A six-month trip into the woods covering 2,168 miles means not only going new places and meeting new people, but it also provides for a revelatory experience. There is something cathartic about being tired, hungry and in the pursuit of happiness. When someone decides to explore the dragons of their soul in the serenity of the wilderness, the real world is shocked, but the adventurer knows that deep understanding takes time, patience and, maybe most of all, separation from the pressures of the daily routine.

The protagonist of the story is Pat Pittard. On the trail, Pat was one of those guys who exuded optimism and confidence, and it didn't take long for the rest of us to discover that this tall, white-cap wearing Southerner had seen the world most of us never would. For many years, Pat was the CEO of a publicly traded company and served on several boards, including serving as chairman of the University of Georgia Foundation. However, the timing of his departure from the corporate world could not have been better. Enron had just exploded, Global Crossing flat lined and WorldCom was heading towards a train wreck and a meeting with the Senate Committee on Ethics.

And most defining as a historic book-marker, teams of misguided religious fundamentalists hijacked commercial airplanes and flew them into history.

As these disasters ricocheted, Pat wandered down the aisle at REI debating the merits of a down sleeping bag with an incredulous 20-year-old sales clerk who couldn't believe this mid-fifties never-been-in-a-tent-before rookie was going to attempt to thru-hike the AT. The young clerk was not the only one looking askance at our would-be hero; his family and friends were speechless.

I met Pat in Central Virginia. We hiked off and on together all the way to Gorham, NH, and I can say I never saw him have a down moment. Naturally, he had his share of setbacks, but his demeanor was always positive and forward looking. Each time our paths would cross, he would holler out "Hey Pipe Wrench," and we would immediately catch up on the latest trail news. Like all of our hiking friends, he was genuinely excited about being on this adventure and just reveled in the "current" of the odyssey.

Now let's turn our attention to the physical attributes of the Appalachian Trail. Its southern terminus is located in Georgia atop Springer Mountain, and the northern terminus is Katahdin in Maine. The trail weaves together fourteen east coast states, with the changes from one state to the next so subtle that a hiker takes a much more blended assessment of the differences in the regions. A thru-hiker will cross the head waters of the Chattahoochee, and rivers like the Potomac, the Hudson and the Delaware. Along with these rivers, a hiker will traverse at least eleven national forests and parks and tread along mountain ranges with names like the Blue Ridge, the Smokies, the Shenandoahs, the Berkshires, the Green Mountains, the Whites and the Mahoosucs, only to name a few. In addition to the rivers and mountain ranges, AT hikers will also come within a few miles of Camp David, thirty miles of Manhattan, and live in communities like Hot Springs, North Carolina; Erwin, Tennessee; Kent, Connecticut; and Monson, Maine.

Hiking the Appalachian Trail means something different to each hiker: to the 20-year-old English major from Vermont, the trail meant living free, having fun, and focusing on the moment and not the goal; to the 30-year-old public school teacher with degrees from Stanford and Harvard, the hike was a totally self-defined process; to the couple from Madison, Wisconsin, the AT was a collective goal to be accomplished together; and finally for the 67-year-old wanderer, the AT allowed him to more fully understand his existence. All of these different experiences and meanings may have one common theme, and Joseph Campbell describes it in the book *The Power of Myth.*

"People say that what we're all seeking is an experience of being alive, so that our life experiences on the purely physical plane will have resonances within our own innermost being and reality, so that we actually feel the nature of being alive." So there it is; we all sought the rapture of being alive.

How does an adventure allow us to feed the rapture? I believe the answer lies in two words—pain and suffering. It is a cliché, but pain and suffering define our human experience because they force us to shed our vanities and admit our mortality in a way that cannot be felt in the daily routine and security of the real world. If you want to feel refreshed, go to a spa or to a resort, but if you want to feel the rapture of being alive, you must endure hardships in the pursuit of a worthy end. However, there are two problems with this "root canal" mentality. One, regardless of the promised end, no one knowingly seeks pain and suffering, or as one of Pat's closest friends told me several months subsequent to Pat finishing the trail, "After seeing that beautiful lake house of his, it's hard to see how Pat could have wanted to live in a tent for six months." Fortunately, the hook is so deeply embedded in the romance of the adventure that we never give enough weight to the presumed pain. Thus, only after you get your feet wet do you fully grasp the hardships that await you. Secondly, after realizing the miscalculation, why not stop? For this I have no answer. The overwhelming majority do stop and now I'm sure they regret it.

Finally, the feeling of being alive, at its deepest level, is mystical. It is an encompassing, unified, ineffable understanding. For me, it is akin to hearing the ninth symphony of Beethoven or it is what Beethoven communicates in his last string quartets: a resolve, a satisfied resignation— "It must be!" Oddly enough, in Pat's original e-mails, the basis for his book that he transmitted contemporaneously from the trail, he says that he hears a deep music in the background of his soul. At around this same time, a fellow hiker mentioned to me that Pat seemed different today, almost melancholy. I believe his inner journey had ended; he had articulated the answer to the question that had followed him some 1,850 miles. The remaining miles, except for the final five he hiked with his wife, would be done simply to achieve a goal, a rather anticlimactic moment in light of what he had already felt.

In life we are always faced with choices. Pat Pittard could have refused the call to hike the Appalachian Trail. In *The Hero of a Thousand Faces,* Joseph Campbell talks about the "refusal of the call."

> "Often in actual life, and not infrequently in the myths and popular tales, we encounter the dull case of the call unanswered; for it is always possible to turn the ear to other interests. Refusal of the summons converts the adventure into its negative. Walled in boredom, hard work, of 'culture,' the subject loses the power to significant affirmative action and becomes the victim to be saved. His flowering world becomes a wasteland of dry stones and his life feels meaningless..."

This is why I think Pat hiked the Appalachian Trail. He feared the inner "wasteland of dry stones."

TABLE OF CONTENTS

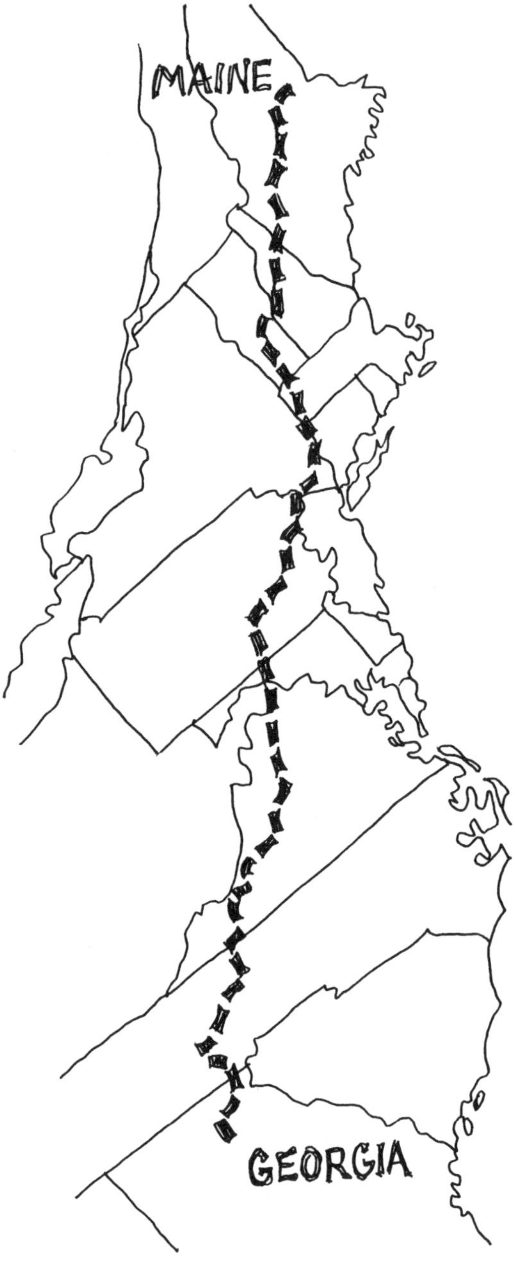
MAINE
GEORGIA

BearFoot
A Northbounder
E-mails from the Appalachian Trail

PATRICK PITTARD

Illustrations by Lisa Chalmers

Now I see the secret
of the making of the best persons.
It is to grow in the open air and
to eat and sleep with the Earth.

—Walt Whitman
"Song of the Open Road"

SECTION ONE

Five Months Later

Three straight days of hard, hot hiking without a shower left me ripe. The unemployed paper worker not only picked me up hitchhiking—when he probably shouldn't—but also went out of his way to bring me here. I wished I didn't smell so badly.

"It really isn't far," he said, pointing up a neglected road. "Go to the end of the road, turn to the left, and you'll see the landing strip."

"I can't thank you enough, please let me chip in for the gas."

He wouldn't hear of it. He smiled and tipped his Red Sox cap. The truck jerked once then moved out and soon disappeared.

It was all quiet here. And became more and more quiet as I reached the end of the road. I saw the landing strip. The mile or so of concrete runway was deserted. When the two paper plants were in full production, the airport was busy. Private planes landed and took off. My driver told me the airport even had a commercial flight once a day. All was silent now. So silent that sounds you normally never hear could be clearly heard. The light wind. A leaf skittering along the concrete in front of me.

Hiking on a paved road was different. You don't look at your feet. You walk more than you hike. I hate gnarly trails, but even more, I detest hiking on paved roads. I reached the airstrip entrance. The chain link fence was open; no one was around.

What do I do now?

I walk to the end of the runway, and I see that I am surrounded by mountains. Down past the end of the runway about 30 miles is Mount Washington. I can't see him now, but I can feel that he is there.

I sling off my backpack, pull out the murder mystery I've been reading, and lay down in the border grass to read. The murder mystery is mostly gone, physically gone, because as all hikers do, I throw away the pages I have read. You never carry extra weight when you're a thru-hiker.

It is hot, early August in New Hampshire. Record highs. But the sky is clear. I read on. I stink so badly my eyes water.

I can't concentrate on the book, so I lay there doing something I was incapable of doing five months ago—I do nothing. I lay there quietly looking at the clouds.

Sometime later, I am not sure how much later, there is a dot in the sky. I watch as it takes shape. I can hear it now. A few minutes later it passes over my head. Sleek and gleaming, it circles and lines up with the airstrip. It touches down, moving away from me. I stand up. The jet turns and heads back.

I knew then I was changed. Forever. Of course changed physically from the months of wear that made some parts of my middle-aged body weaker and other parts stronger. But much more, and profoundly, changed in the way I saw the world and my place in it. At that moment, with perfect clarity, I could look back on a life half spent (a successful life by any modern measure) and see so many possibilities ignored. So many paths not taken. So many opportunities to step into the glare of pure truth, and so many occasions of choosing the grayness of compromise that is both the blessing and curse of successful business. More importantly, I also saw a new kind of living that I had never considered before.

But we are ahead of ourselves. Let's go back to the beginning.

"Well, what do you need?"
"Everything."

I had never hiked—never. I had never slept in a tent I pitched. I was as raw a rookie as ever left Springer Mountain. I cooked in a stove upside down for the first few nights. I slept in my sleeping bag inside out for 400 miles. All—and I do mean all—of my gear was new. Most of it was still in its plastic wrappers. My boots were certainly not broken in, nor did I have much more than a passing understanding of what that meant.

Compared to me, Bill Bryson, who wrote the blockbuster book about hiking the AT, reveling in his ignorance, was a grizzled veteran.

I was an out-of-shape ex-CEO whose last true physical exertion was 40 years earlier on a high school football field. The first time I picked up my fully-weighted backpack, I found simply to stay upright was not a gimme. The pack actually hurt as I walked around. The kid, who put the 45 pounds of weight into the pack I was trying out, watched me with open concern. God bless her, she didn't want me to hurt myself right there in the store.

The outfitter clerks found me hard to hear. I adopted this embarrassed mumble whenever I spoke.

"Where will you be hiking?"
"The Appalachian Trail," I would mumble—definitely with no eye contact.

"What section?"
Lower volume: "All of it."
There were often long pauses after my responses.

"When will you be leaving?"
"Mid-February."

Open mouth then, "Well, what do you need?"
Almost inaudible now: "Everything."

We stood staring at each other for what seemed to be a full minute. Her mouth moved, but no sound came out.

Many hours later as I left the store with a shopping cart overfilled, the employees lined the window as I crossed the parking lot.

That night I tried out my one-man tent. I told my wife, Dana, not to let me back into the house. "I'm going into the wilderness."

Between our house and the tennis court, I put up the tent. The hardest part is feeding the aluminum spines through their sleeves so the tent will stand up. The next twenty minutes is like a rerun of *I Love Lucy*. But I get it up, throw my sleeping bag inside, and settle into my tent for the night.

"Pat?" Dana says. "Pat?" Again and a pause. "Pat? Darlin'?" She is hanging out the upstairs window.

"Dana, I can't talk to you, I'm in the wilderness."

"But did you hear those noises? I think a car had a wreck out front."

"I'm in the wilderness."

"The TV says it's going down into the twenties."

"I can't talk to you, I'm in the wilderness."

She quietly closes the window. She is right, it's cold as shit.
I crawl into my sleeping bag.

Why? Why would a 56-year-old man, who is not a hiker, choose to hike nearly 2,200 miles? I will get to that, but first I will explain my method of recording this journey.

It was fairly simple, really. When I reached camp at night, I jotted down events—but mostly my impressions—on a tiny spiral notebook. When I found a hard-line phone some days later, I would dictate my "chapters" to my former assistant, Tracy Jones Keiser. Tracy is also one of my closest and dearest friends, and she *wanted* to do this. Go figure.

She would pick up my dictation on a voice mail system we shared and, pretty much unedited and undrafted, would send out the journal to an e-mail distribution. This e-mail list grew over time to a substantial number of family, friends, and acquaintances.

It was then sent out by them to a second generation of readers; folks I had never met. Even a fifth grade class followed the trip. Once I discovered this, I tried to clean up my language a bit.

I became fairly naked as a personality during this process. The physical and emotional exertion required begins to peel off the protective layers that civilization creates. The wilderness is dirty and wet and hot and freezing. It stings, scratches, cuts, and hurts. Your hands and legs cramp. The water isn't perfect, and the food—at least what I fixed—is terrible. Your body rebels then restructures inside and out; it requires you to shape up. It becomes leaner and stronger.

Your emotions go through the same process. Your hiking buddies know you better than friends you have known for decades. There is next to no privacy. Pretense is impossible. And your performance is obvious, no need for interpretation.

So as I sent e-mails, I found it increasingly easy to expose myself, often in a not very flattering way. This was a new experience for me. I had been a person who seldom let his emotions show, so much so that I wasn't sure I even felt them anymore.

The journal served another function. It kept me in touch with my friends; it made me feel their presence. It made me stay alert to what I saw and felt because I wanted all of the readers to share what I experienced. Also it served as a chronicle, helping me remember. For all these reasons, I was more observant to my surroundings. This journal enhanced each day's hike.

I didn't write every day. I seldom actually wrote about hiking, although it made up 80 percent of my waking time.

When I started, I didn't know why I was out there. This came into focus as the many months and thousands of miles poured through the system that was me.

GA›ME

GAME. In hiker language that means Georgia to Maine. It means you are a Northbounder trying to complete the longest hiking trail on earth, the Appalachian Trail. The AT is to hikers as Everest is to climbers. It is serious stuff—not a "game" at all. Thousands attempt it; in a good year, a few hundred finish. In a tough year, many less. This year, 2002, has been, and is, a tough year.

Those who attempt the entire Trail in one year carry the almost exalted title, "thru-hiker." If they fail, and stop for any reason, and don't complete the Trail within twelve months, the title is self-stripped. If they ever wish to be called thru-hiker again, they must start back at the beginning. To pick up where they left off sometime in the future is called section hiking.

A section-hiker is respected.

A thru-hiker is revered.

In a hiker bar, to reveal you thru-hiked the AT creates a sense of awe. Elvis is in the building.

Thru-hikers easily recognize each other. Their faces, their boots, and how they carry their packs. The weathered, but functional look of their gear. But mostly it is in their stride. Their stride is athletic, not a walk at all. The stride is long and efficient. There is no jangling, no wasted motion; if a thru-hiker has change in his pocket, you will never hear it when he strides.

All one has to do to adopt the title is begin. The challenge is not gaining the title, but keeping it. If you finish, forever, you are a thru-hiker. Your resume will read: AT Thru-Hiker '02.

You don't have to be chosen to attempt to thru-hike the AT. You don't have to prove yourself on shorter, easier trails. Here you can play in the Super Bowl without ever having been in the play-offs.

It is mostly a young person's pursuit. Most are under 30. A great majority are under 40. But there are retirees and otherwise freed-up older folks. And while we make up a smaller percentage at the beginning, we represent a healthier ratio at the end. Maybe we "oldsters" have more experience with pain and tenacity.

The numbers are never kept, but it seems most successful thru-hikers finish solo. Although a majority start in groups of two or more.

Northbounder. This word creates an emotional, almost visceral reaction when I hear it. It is my direction, my goal, my identity. It felt good to be a Northbounder. Not only was I proud to be one, but I was also proud to be among the others who were. We were together on a great adventure. Northbounder also reminds me of the term "true north." It is a compass setting which does not waver. There is no "almost true north" on the compass. It is or it isn't. True north also means the unbridled truth. Thru-hiking means all of it. These two are absolute terms. Uncompromising—complete. The best outcome would be for us to always be Northbounders and thru-hikers in some small, special way.

E-mail #1

February 26, 2002

This is Bearfoot, my first report.

It is required on the Appalachian Trail to have a trail name. This is the name I will be known by to all my hiking colleagues. Dana and I spent a lot of time trying to come up with something applicable, and we finally came up with "Bearfoot." I collect carved bears; a hike is on foot. Ta-da!

Pre-AT

The AT is the longest hiking-only trail in the world, 2,168 miles—it goes through 14 states and has altitudes ranging from almost sea level to almost 7,000 feet. The AT connects the peaks of the Appalachian Mountains up and down, up and down. *I can do it. Most importantly, if my body—particularly my back—holds together, I can do it. I must think I can, and say I can.*

Pre-AT is all—I repeat all—about the pack, the backpack and what is in it and what is strapped on it. The 35–50 pounds straps mostly to your hips and is guided by your back and shoulders. 35 pounds is a lot of weight. But, few people get by with only having 35 pounds; still that's my goal. At present, without water, my pack weighs 38 pounds, but I am carrying a lot of cold weather gear that I won't have to carry later. Water will add several pounds.

Mostly the weight decides how miserable you are, and where. A lot of weight, you are miserable on the Trail, but comfortable in camp. A little weight, you are more comfortable on the Trail, but miserable in camp.

With more weight, you will have what you should have in an emergency. But the more weight you carry, the more likely you are to have an emergency.

Pre AT—the biggest purchase is boots. Number two, the backpack.

I have settled on Asolo boots and an Osprey backpack—both for the same reasons—comfort and weight. Clothes? No natural fabrics except wool socks. Synthetic underwear—yuck—but there you go.

Most common questions:

Are you going with a group?
Why are you doing this?
Are you taking a weapon?
Are you taking a cell phone?
What are you going to read first?

Answers:

I am going alone.
If you ask, I can't explain it. No, and yes. *A World Lit Only by Fire.*
I will miss you all terribly—and hope you will join me for some small part. I'll cook!
Next, Springer Mountain to the first camp.

E-mail #2–Map Marker #1

A slick stone . . .

Dana, my wife, and I are going to Amicalola Falls State Park Tuesday night and have a big breakfast Wednesday morning the 27th. Then I will start off. I registered at the visitor's center as a thru-hiker. The little gray-haired ranger lady made us as unwelcome as possible. She must have received training as an airline flight attendant.

I wanted to make sure we could find the Forest Service Road, so we made a dry run to Springer Tuesday afternoon. It was crisp and clear. The Georgia mountains were naked of leaves, opening the visibility to us.

The sun was out, but it was very cold. Tonight should be in the 20s or even teens. We found our way easily. Our car was the only one in the car park. We saw our first blaze—a small white mark on a tree, two inches by six inches, and realized we were on the AT. We backtracked from where we were parked .9 miles, and we were at the beginning point of the Appalachian Trail. The views were spectacular.

We were the only people there. It would have been easy to miss this famous spot. There was a plaque that blended with the rocks and vegetation. I signed the Trail book, which was in a steel box underneath a rock. I used my trail-name for the first time on the Trail. After signing *Bearfoot,* I drew a little picture of a paw print, something I would do hundreds of times in the months to come. As I looked out over the Appalachian Mountains, I knew I couldn't go back to Amicalola.

After so much anticipation, I couldn't leave the AT now.

I had to get started.

Again, for the thousandth time, Dana understood. She kissed me on the cheek and headed back up the Trail toward the car park. Dana is a strong, confident woman. But she is not a pain in the ass about it. She is a happy person. One friend calls her "a sweetie." Dana senses I need a moment of solitude.

Tallulah patiently sat with me here at the start. One little paw on my leg. I picked up a slick stone. It was the size of a quarter, smooth, almost blue in color. It had no business being here; it wasn't indigenous. I slipped it in the baggie that held my money, and Tallulah and I caught up with Dana.

It was late, maybe 4 p.m. when I left the car park with a 43-pound pack and a walking stick. I kissed Dana, and later Tallulah, good-bye and headed north.

I got approximately 4 miles up the AT. The Trail had been totally and completely mine. I met no one. I camped beside a small waterfall, tent up. It wasn't too hard. The special matches that will light when they are wet, don't light at all. I wore out the striker. Luckily I had a fifty-nine cent BIC, and I was able to light my stove. I cooked an envelope of my freeze-dried trail food. Drank water. Scooped up some more water and boiled it for tomorrow.

I ate a bit, it started getting very cold, and I crawled into my sleeping bag.

This is how I signed my name hundreds of times in the Trail registers

Springer to Neel's Gap—"Aye McTavish—weather permittin'."

The next two nights have record lows in Georgia. Where I am, it is 12 degrees overnight.

The second night, I sleep with five humans and a dog named Annie at Gooch shelter. Annie and I cuddle up.

The night before, I was in my tent and awoke to snow. Dana met me where the AT crossed a paved road at Woody Gap. This night I slept in a bed—pretty spiffy. I'll really miss seeing her as I move north, and she goes home to Atlanta.

She brings me back the next morning, and I disappear from her sight into the forest. The view at the top of Blood Mountain is more than fabulous. I am there alone; it is hard to believe, as this is the second most visited mountain on the entire AT. I sit in a historic rock shelter and eat a Powerbar. This shelter, it is rumored, will be destroyed this summer because it is too close to a dirt road and has become a drug hang-out. Sad.

The Appalachians are a billion—give or take—years old. They are rounded by the winds and rain. Much older than the more dramatic Rockies or the Alps. Those mountains did not exist when the amphibians crawled ashore—but the Appalachians stood there to greet the pre-mammals that did.

Tomorrow I will hike 15 miles in the continuing ice and rain, most likely, to Low Gap. Dana has continued to be fabulous.

Buddy, my brother, will be pleased to know that the first joke I told to thru-hikers was one of his. It was about two Scottish caddies who carried golf bags through the foul weather of Northern Scotland. Rain, ice, and half-frozen snot ran down their faces. One asked the other if he would see him tomorrow. "Aye, McTavish—weather permittin'."

— Neels Gap, also known as Walasi-Ye —

E-mail #2 (continued)–**Map Marker #3**

Neel's to Low Gap

Fifty percent of all thru-hikers quit by Neel's Gap, I am told.

Neel's is the only place where the Trail goes through a building.

It is a classical, rock building with a top-flight outfitter inside. The outfitter's job is to sell you all new shit and mail home all the old shit REI sold you two weeks ago.

Normally, thru-hikers stay in the hostel downstairs. It is a series of bunk beds, flushing toilets, dueling snoring. But I have Dana and don't stay there. We stay in a small cabin down the road.

Back at Neel's the next morning, I leave her at 6:45 a.m.

It is raining as I leave. It gets worse. Colder. Driving rain. Then sleet. My gloves are worthless—soaked and cold. My boots are full. Waterproof Gore-Tex working in reverse. Keeping the water in. The Trail is alternatively slippery rock and sliding mud. While I only make it to Low Gap shelter, I am happy to be out of the weather. I am the first one there. Given the weather, I expect more hikers. It would be tough in a tent tonight. The shelter fills up—all really good guys. We have great conversations.

It's hard to find out normal background information about your fellow hikers. Nobody talks much about where they are from and what they "did." Asking that is somewhat like a prison question, "Whatcha in for Looee?" No one cares, and neither should I. I am a hiker now. A thru-hiker. Nothing else matters.

I write to all of you and turn off my forehead light.

– I write to all of you –

Map Marker #4

Rocks as big as a Volkswagen

I tell myself if I make it to Unicoi by 1 p.m., I will press on to Tray Mountain.

What a horrible day. My feet hurt. Everything hurts. I tried to sleep last night beside the only guy who could put David Chalmers' snoring to shame. David is my brother-in-law. When he snores, he can vibrate a vase off the living room coffee table. But compared to this guy, David is a beginner. His trail-name is *Drifter*.

Today, I went through Boulder Fields. These rocks are as big as a Volkswagen Beetle and as small as a football. When you step on one you don't know if it's going to be a solid step, or slippery. It's all on faith. Ankles, feet, legs, and hips—everything pounds. I can't find water. Strange when you consider all the rain. I need a spring. Clean water—springs don't need treating. I think the iodine is upsetting my stomach from treating bad water. Giardia is bad stuff. Giardia is usually a lifetime problem once you contract it. It tears up your digestive system. You can die of it, but most often you do not. At the very least, it will end your hike. It is caused by what is deposited in the water, not the water itself. Get it? So it doesn't matter how clean the water looks.

Dehydration is a hiker's constant enemy. To find and clean and carry and drink, and find and clean and carry and drink ... this cycle never ends, and becomes a severe problem often. Water sources become priority one to all thru-hikers. These sources are listed in your Data Book, the most important written thing you carry. It points you right or left to find the precious liquid.

Everything seems uphill. Is that possible? Every step kills. The springs are frozen. Finally, I find some water. The Trail turns downhill and I turn it on. But, I turn it on carefully because a fall by yourself is not a good thing.

I arrive at Unicoi Gap and Highway 75; it is 1:45 p.m. Shit! I don't want to negotiate the sheer cliff approach to the Tray Mountain Shelter in the dark. Another hard freeze warning is predicted plus possible sleet, and I don't have my tent this section. I mailed it forward thinking I would make shelters the next couple of days. Three miles back to a shelter—five miles forward to another. I walk to the side of the road and stick out my thumb. A trail angel stops—probably only the sixth or seventh car to pass me. He drives a beautiful, spotless Suburban. I am covered with mud. "No problem," he says, "it cleans." What a miracle! Why did he stop?

He is going through Helen and asks where do I want to be dropped? I tell him any motel with a fast food place next door. My angel drops me at the Best Western—$51—KFC and Taco Bell contiguous. A very tough day ends well.

Sixteen miles tomorrow.

E-mail #3

Characters

I came off the Trail for two days. I will explain later. I am back now.

Characters. In the short time I have been on the Trail, I have already met some real characters.

Maine-ah. Maine-ah is probably 70, full beard, no teeth. He is "walking home." Simply cannot shut-up. Walking, sitting, eating—he always talks. I love Maine-ah. He has an incredibly small pack and seems to be wearing sweat pants. It was 12 degrees the last time I saw him.

Healed. Healed was sick and now he is healed, so, of course, his Trail name is Healed. Annie is his large, mixed-breed dog. Annie talks more than Healed. Annie bunked with me at Gooch Shelter. That dog has put in 8,000 miles on the AT. And they are on their way again. The AT belongs to Healed and Annie, and they belong to it. All the work to preserve the AT is justified if only these two souls walked it.

Miz Gorp thru-hiked twenty years ago. She is back with *Chase*, her friend and hiking companion. The two of them are a great help to me without openly asking why such a dumb ass is here on the Trail. They explained that if I cook with my stove right-side up, it might work better. Very diplomatic.

Dwayne Drifter is carrying his Bible from Texas. His wife leaves little notes in the Bible. He loves that so much, but he cannot read them because he lost his glasses on the Trail. So I read them to Dwayne. They are sweet—so sweet. I was out of water one afternoon and turned the corner on the Trail and there stood Dwayne Drifter, taking a big swig from a liter bottle. "How about some water?" Dwayne offered. "Take as much as you want, I've just filtered some." Dwayne carries his Bible—and he lives it too.

There were the three runners. The day it rained so much, and I stopped for the day at Low Gap Shelter, three runners splashed up and in the shelter. Great outfits, tight pants, fluorescent shoes and little back packs. A muddy slob like me really wanted to hate these guys. They told me they run about 100 miles of the AT from time to time. They hope to finish the entire AT in 10–15 years. As they leave to finish their section, each of them reaches in his pack and hands me a beer. "Man!" was all I could say. "Man!" I said it a second time. They laugh and slosh off.

There is *Blink* the anesthesiologist, and *Stevareno* with his horrible blisters. I wonder how he is doing.

Because I left the Trail for two days, I will lose contact with these guys but meet others. It is clear now that this hike will be full of characters. My guess is that someone is writing in a journal about the old guy, who knows nothing about hiking, hasn't got a clue, and thinks he is going to thru-hike the AT.

E-mail #4–Map Marker #5

The Doo-Wop Boys at Muskrat Shelter

The last two days have been tough, very tough. But I get down the Trail 28 miles. That's a lot of miles for a beginner.

Wednesday was awful. I don't want to talk about it.

Thursday was better.

I see Annie's paw prints. Makes me feel good.

I reach Blye Gap—one of 14 states completed. I wish I could celebrate. I can't. My spirits are beyond low.

Georgia behind, I enter North Carolina.

The AT is maintained by hiking clubs. The Nantahala Hiking Club (NHC) picks up maintenance at the North Carolina line and the NHC doesn't do shit! Fire these assholes! Trees are on the Trail everywhere (they are called blow downs). And no switchbacks, to get to the top of a knob—straight up. Hand-over-hand in many places.

The shelter at Muskrat Creek is filling up. Three guys I call the *Doo-Wop Boys,* have radio headphones that keep them singing way into the night. We can't hear the music, we can only hear the Doo-Wop Boys, and it's not pretty. I consider multiple homicides. I don't know if my bitching is because of the situation, or my problem—it's probably me.

Yesterday my spirit died. Today it's better, but still bad. Tomorrow—hopefully will be close to normal.

This hiking thing is hard to do. Very hard. Your body hurts or is tired everywhere. The hardest, however, is mental. You cross escape routes all too often. A highway or a village. All you have to do is call, and you go home. If you are exhausted and mentally down at an escape route, mental toughness is what is important to avoid the phone call. Step after step up. Noise explosions come out of my mouth. Not quite grunts. Millions of steps to go.

Sometimes I just stop. Dead on the Trail. I put my two hands on my friend—my walking stick—and put my forehead on my hands. And I just stop. Then in a minute, I go again. I must raise my spirits. I must.

A quick physical check up. I tried glasses and everything was much too foggy. I am on to contacts. My lips are chapped beyond anything you have ever seen. My back is cooperating. My left knee really hurts. Feet will need a whole separate e-mail. My hands claw-up at night from carrying my walking stick all day. I put a lot of weight on that stick. My stick is my friend. My weight is down, I don't know how much. My hips hurt where my legs attach. Overall, though, I am okay.

—The Flying Pork Chop.
Our walking yardsale —

E-mail #5

I meet the Flying Porkchop.

I pass a guy back in Georgia going up Tray Mountain. He is easily 250 pounds. His pack is at least another 60. This is not a sport for out-of-shape dudes pushing 310 pounds up 5,000 feet of elevation, but there is something fetching about this guy. When I blow past someone, he is really going slowly. I thought in my mind—not a chance.

As I pass him, I raise a hand, "I'm Bearfoot." He stops, his face lit up, "I'm the *Flying Porkchop*."

I cannot get him out of my mind.

Pebbles in my boot. Shit. Shit. This hiking stuff is hard. Very hard. It's harder than anything I had ever done. Endlessly forcing my legs to take one more upward step. I hear my heart beating in my ears. My breath comes out in gasps. Sweat, even in twenty-degree weather, drips in my eyes. Straps rub raw all over the place. My feet hurt like nothing I have ever experienced, but I keep stepping and stepping. And I know there are hours, days, weeks, and months more of this. And now, I have a fucking pebble in my boot. I have to stop, find a place to sit, take off my pack, and take off my gaiters—a synthetic form of spats and very difficult to remove. Then I must untie mud-encrusted laces, dig around in the boot and find that goddamn menace that makes my hiking hell. I am not happy.

As I am doing all this, I hear clinking, clanking and puffing coming up the hill. It is that walking yard sale I passed this morning, I swear if he says, "Got a pebble?" I will kill him.

"Bearfoot! Taking a break?" What a smile. I have to giggle.

Then the Flying Porkchop sits down beside me and we get to know each other. His goodwill is infectious. He lifts my spirits.

Three days later, I am a mile from a legendary AT stopover, Rainbow Springs. It is pouring—I mean pouring—about 3:00 p.m. and very dark. To get to Rainbow Springs, I hike down a deserted highway made obsolete by one of the new four-laners 3 miles north and parallel. Up in the distance, I see a figure coming my way. Moving up hill, I recognize Pork Chop.

"Bearfoot! Heading to Rainbow?"

"Damn Porky" I said, "you look good." And he did.

In such a short time, it looks like he has dropped 15 pounds, has a more reasonable pack, and he is heading out, leaving the bunkhouse—a warm and dry place—and getting a head start on tomorrow morning.

"Chili is great, tell Jensine I said hello. See you down the Trail, Bearfoot."

I stand in the downpour and watch the Flying Pork Chop head up the hill to the AT intersection.

Rainbow Springs is great. A wonderful and unique wilderness everything store and hiker's hostel. The chili is made by Jensine herself. Jensine is a small and warm person, but with lots and lots of opinions. "Jensine for President," I say.

The next morning I take my first real spill. A complete flat-faced, body-length, sprawled-out spill. Once you start to fall with a full backpack, you are going down. My toes struck a stumble-stump. A stumble-stump is a cutoff sapling about 2 inches from the ground, hiding under a leaf. These bastards are deadly. My head misses a boulder by about 6 inches.

For the first time, I am afraid. I climb the sheer rock face of Albert Mountain in a hard rain. This is not time for a foot to slip. I am tired, and the rock is wet. There is nothing behind me but air. Most terrifying, I am alone. A fall late in the day would not be good. I make it safely, and because of the rain, again, choose to stay in a shelter.

Those of us who have come this far have added the passing of Neel's Gap, completed Georgia, and passed our first 100 miles. We are officially thru-hikers!

At least four million people step on the AT any given year. Approximately 4,000 start as thru-hikers. Ten percent of those become 2,000-Milers. You must finish the AT entirely to get the coveted 2,000-Miler patch, which really commemorates the entire AT, 2,168 miles.

I have a long way to go, but the first steps are at least behind me, and I am a thru-hiker.

E-mail #6–Map Marker #6

Nantahala Outdoor Center (NOC)

Cold to start. But a good day to hike.

I hike from Old 64 over a small mountain and get to New 64. There is Chase, dropping off Miz Gorp. Chase is a fabulous thru-hiker. He already has his 2,000-Miler badge. But this time he isn't thru-hiking, just doing the first section, Springer to Franklin. He says he has some work that he has to get back to, and I said, "Getting back to the real world?" He looks at me still and straight: "Bearfoot, where you are going is the real world." He gives me an apple and a handshake and drives off.

Miracles happen. What can you say about a miracle? It's about 1 p.m. and I am about to ascend Wayah Bald. My stomach is grumbling—my lower stomach—and I start looking right and left. You are supposed to be at least 50 feet off the Trail when nature calls—dig a hole, commune with nature, and fill the hole back.

As I am checking for an appropriate place, I spot, not 60 yards away, a little house—an outhouse. In it is a roll of paper. Miles from nowhere, I stumble upon a little church camp closed for the winter, but they obviously keep their outhouses open for hikers. This is as great as the three runners who brought the beer.

While I am completing my task, I read the graffiti on the walls. There are obviously a number of thru-hikers who have been here. GAtoME I see several times. Also a little poem. "Here I sit broken hearted, I need to shit, but I only farted." This obviously wasn't one of my most mature colleagues. As I start to leave, I see scribbled in the corner of the door—"fuck you." How incredibly sad that was—that this person would leave this epitaph to anyone and everyone. Someone who feels so lost that all who pass need to be cursed. So sad. I wish for you, my friend, better days.

On to Wayah. Very, very high, all afternoon will be up hill. I put my pack back on and start.

Wayah is a test of endurance. While it is very steep, it's never hand over hand, but relentless, consistently and constantly up. When I summit, there is a paved road and civilians. I think, "This is my trail! You can't be up here unless you walk up here." As I enter the observation area, all the civilians look me over suspiciously and give me a wide berth.

I approach a rock tower that once was a fire lookout. Four guys in civilian clothes approach me with their Golden, named Hank. "Hey thru-hiker," they called out—making me feel proud. They turn out to be hikers who had climbed this section years ago. They drove it today. We talk and exchange stories. They give me a card so they can get this e-mail.

While on top of the mountain I call Dana. She has been down; not something common in her. She is doing better, so I feel better, too. Dana has been my rock, while I stepped out on this incredibly selfish adventure. If she isn't doing well, it saps my resolve.

By nightfall, I camp in solitude. I should make dinner—but I'm exhausted and do the stupid thing and eat peanuts, and candy, and crackers and I am in my bag by 6:30.

My plan Monday is to have an easy day, stop at a hostel, get a good meal, and hike into Nantahala Outdoor Center on Tuesday. (The NOC should not be confused with the NHC!)

Sir Isaac changes all that. This young, handsome kid, college age, who is going on to the NOC today. "Only 18 miles," he said. I reach the hostel turnoff at 1:00—eight more miles to NOC. I could get there by dark. My cell phone has some service, and I call the NOC and book a room. I am now off on my longest single day. An exhausting day, but stunningly beautiful. At times, I am on a trail at the sheer peak of a mountain, no wider than my walking stick with precipitous drop offs on both sides. There are times I consider taking off my pack and crawling part of the Trail.

Very steep now, all downward, my feet crunch into the front of my boot with every step. Sir Isaac passes me again—he stopped for lunch.

Why isn't downhill easy? But I get there.

At the NOC, a good friend of mine is the chief financial officer of this white water and outdoors organization. Tom Burns and Susan pick me up and take me to a Mexican restaurant. HEAVEN! We called Dana. Tomorrow I leave the Trail for about two weeks as I go to Cuba.

I will return to the NOC in two weeks—then Fontana, then the very tough Smokies, and always lurking in the future—the Whites.

E-mail #7

Non-equipment folks might want to skip this chapter.

What do you pack when you leave home for seven months?

Food
Water
Clothes
Cooking stuff
Miscellaneous
Home
Furniture
First-aid kit

By the way, keep all this stuff and the pack it sits in under 50 pounds. If you are really good—under 40 pounds. Rule 1—if you don't wash your clothes, you don't need as much.

Thru-hikers stink. No, I don't mean they smell bad. They stink.

You must layer. In the cold, you cannot put it on if you don't have it with you. Lots of synthetics, because they wick perspiration from your body. Natural fabric keeps water close. When you stop walking and the exercise stops, this water heated by your body action cools and this is the first step to hypothermia.

You see no jeans or cotton t-shirts on the Trail. At least not on real hikers. Sometimes a couple of stupid day hikers will be dressed that way, but no one with hiker's I.Q. over 40.

Water is a must, but very heavy. How much do you carry, and how much do you gamble? You can gamble that you will find some on the Trail. But it is not funny to be short of water, and then come upon some that is suspicious. Dehydration is not only a summertime problem; water will always be a hiker's most pressing need. Treating water takes one of three things: filtering equipment which is bulky and heavy, time for chemicals to work, or time and fire for boiling. Time and weight are your enemies.

You must have a stove of some sort. The choices are infinite. Some sound like jet aircraft when they fire up, some are fueled and they have to be "pumped up" in the morning before they will light.

The pumping kind led to a private joke I only shared with myself. I was behind these two guys who were sitting in the shelf with their fuel stove between their legs, and they were pumping fuel. So from behind I saw these guys with their hands between their legs jerking up and down. The sight brought back some memories of my early adolescence, and I broke into laughter. They both turned and stared at me.

Okay back to the stove. There are alcohol units; there are wood burning units, on and on.

An Esbit—about the size of a deck of cards, titanium, feather-light—was my choice. I have accelerant in square packs about the size of a pat of butter. Light the accelerant, put it on the small titanium stove, and it flares up. It can boil water in about four minutes.

I eat yuppie food. It is freeze-dried and in envelopes. You buy it at the outfitter.

Open the envelope, pour in hot water, seal it for a couple of minutes, reopen and eat. And it's almost good. Well, not really. Old-line hikers hate freeze-dried. It is too easy, too fast, and too expensive. An envelope costs between $5 and $10. These guys dehydrate their own food before the hike.

So how do you consume 5,000–6, 000 calories a day to maintain your weight?

Impossible. You lose weight. I carry candy, peanuts, and lots of fatty stuff and I am losing weight fast.

When I hitch into town, I eat like an orphaned Sumo wrestler, and I still lose weight.

For a while this is great. Then it will become a big worry.

House and furniture? Tent and sleeping bag. Both are heavy—five pounds and four pounds, respectively. When the weather warms up, I can get a lighter sleeping bag. Many ditch the tent for a lightweight tarp. There is also "stuff." Do you want to brush your teeth? Take pills? Carry toilet paper? Take pictures? A thru-hikers book I read listed 70 possible items of "stuff."

As precious as every ounce I carry is, I do carry three different trail guides. The Bible of the AT is the *Data Book.* Small and thin, it is written in code that keeps it small and thin. But to hike the AT without it is madness. *The Thru-Hikers Companion* tells you where you can stop, sleep, bunk, get food, find an ATM, and sometimes a little about the area you are in. The ATC offers a series of maps. They differ, sometimes greatly, in format. This is because they are published by the different trail clubs along the way.

I carry a *Data Book,* a *Companion,* and the appropriate map. I mail home the pages of the *Companion* that I have used. I have mailed to me new maps that chart what's up ahead.

When I started, I had my hike planned out weeks in advance. Ridiculous. All the plans got screwed up immediately by rain, blisters, elevation or an opportunity to get a pizza or a pint of Ben & Jerry's. So, it got to the point that my hiking plan was a day or two ahead. I reviewed my *Guide* each night, and referred to my *Data Book* and maps constantly through the day's hike.

Because I hiked alone, I carried more reference materials than many hikers. Also, I couldn't stand not knowing where I was going, or what was ahead. For example, all the maps were much like road maps and gave you a quick picture of how far a shelter, a campsite, or a road crossing would be. But each map also gave you an elevation chart, which told you how much up and down, and how steep that up and down would be. This had the benefit of creating dread. One hiker I saw wore a t-shirt; on the front, "Shit Happens," on the back, "A lot." Up and down is what we dread not how far.

So what we carry, and how much that weighs create a hundred decisions and usually, particularly at the beginning, we carry too much. Weight dictates everything. If you have an accident or blow out a knee or an ankle, it is probably because you carried too much weight. The good news is that while you are groveling in pain, somewhere in your overstuffed pack you will find your trusty emergency whistle and you can blow and blow for help.

A short side story

Something I just discovered lately.

It is a lucky person who has loved ones. And I am lucky.

Remember the terribly cold second night?

My brother, Buddy, could not help being a big brother. After all, he is very good at it.

That night—killer cold—was my first full day on the Trail. I am not an experienced wilderness person. Let me put it this way. I had never—not once—carried a pack or spent a night in the wilderness prior to my first night on the AT. Buddy was appropriately concerned. But by the same token, he ain't no Davey Crockett himself.

So with his jeans and ski coat he decides to pull me off the Trail. Me 56, him 60—he still is my big brother.

How does one find someone on the AT? He had a vague estimate of where I was. In his Cadillac, he began cutting through dirt forest roads. Whistling our secret whistle, he carries a thermos of coffee and a sack of steak biscuits. The rescue begins.

Stop a moment. I have prepared and have the proper clothes, sleeping bag, and emergency equipment. Buddy is on forest roads, in a Cadillac, in jeans.

Who is in the greatest danger?

Shockingly, I find out later, he actually came within two miles of where I sheltered for the night. The night I slept with Annie the dog. Buddy did find an AT shelter, and a thru-hiker. Fittingly, this hiker had the Trail name *Lone Ranger.* His real name is Lewis. He was the recipient of the coffee and steak biscuits.

Much later, I find out about the attempted rescue mission.

My hero. Is this guy great or what? I'm glad he came out of it in one piece.

E-mail #8

A short recess–Havana, Cuba

The oldest building in the Western Hemisphere, still standing in its original form, is in Havana. It is a rock structure, part of a fortress, in the old town. It was built in the mid-1500s by the Spanish.

It sits on a spot where teams of horses pulled a wooden chain from the floor of Havana Harbor. This chain would snag ships trying to sneak into the harbor at night.

The Spaniards rank right up there in historical atrocities and genocide. They eradicated entire races of people in Central and South America, most notably the Incas. The Incas' spears were no match for the Conquistadors' gunpowder. And these efficient murderers wiped out thousands of people using only a couple of hundred of their own soldiers.

What for?

Gold.

Where was this stolen gold collected and counted?

Havana.

When gold is concentrated in one spot, who shows up? Pirates. So Havana was a walled city. Each night on a boat out in the harbor, a cannon was fired at 8:00 p.m. The gates were closed and the chain was pulled up into the harbor. No one could leave or enter the city after 8:00 p.m. Any ship that was tangled in the chain was blown to kingdom come the next morning.

My vote for the most efficient murderers at this point in history is the Spanish. The master killer was Christopher Columbus. Even though, technically, he was not

Spanish, he sailed under the Spanish flag, and established a murderous trend. There was a lot of good competition, but in the Olympic slaughtering competition, Spain wins the gold. Figuratively and actually.

The cannon is still shot each night, a sad tradition perpetuated.

Cubans are fascinating people. Very complex, and normally I would love sinking my teeth into their culture. But this had taken me from the Trail, and I am distracted. I need to get back to the mountains of North America.

Great Britain took Havana away from the Spanish a few centuries later. They decided not to sail into the harbor and get the shit blown out of themselves. Duh. Parking east of Havana, marching west, they took the city from the rear fairly easily. Once they had it, they couldn't, for the life of themselves, figure out why, so they swapped Havana back to the Spanish for Florida.

I am going to swap Havana, too, for North Carolina. I am here in Cuba because pre-hike, I promised to accompany a University of Georgia group. But I must get back to the AT.

Back to NOC, Fontana Dam soon, the Smokies after that, and a little R&R at Hot Springs, North Carolina.

E-mail #9–Map Markers #7 and #8

Return to Nantahala Outdoor Center (NOC)

Return to the Trail.

Tom and Susan Burns continue their fabulous hospitality. Dana and I stay with them, and Susan makes a spaghetti dinner. Tom takes me to the trailhead and pulls off one more special gift. He arranges to have my backpack delivered to me 14 miles down the Trail. This is called "slack-packing." Slack-packing is a hiker's nirvana.

On top of that, Tom has the job done by Aurelia Kennedy, the original founder of NOC. Aurelia—who I had never met before—picks up my pack from Tom at about 2:00 p.m., and drives to Stecoah Gap to meet me. She arrives early—and actually comes up the Trail an hour and hikes back to Stecoah with me, my first walking companion. She slows down often to let me catch up. She is 66 and is hiking the AT in sections. Over the years, she and some of her friends hiked 100–200 miles each year. She has hiked the AT all except for 133 miles—33 in New York, 100 in Virginia. She will finish this summer. She started this section hiking in 1987.

We say our good-byes at Stecoah, and I hike a very hard 2½ miles to Brown Fork Gap. This is where I put up for the night. Weather is a hard freeze tonight. I'll put on all the clothing I have with me, and ball up in my sleeping bag. I put my water bladder in my sleeping bag with me, so it doesn't freeze. Please warm up.

Here at Brown Fork, I run into *Motor Mouth,* my trail-name for the machine-gun giggler. You know, when someone giggles to punctuate every sentence? "Boy that mountain was tough, hee hee hee hee hee." Sometimes they use it to soften a naturally tactless nature. "Boy your pack is sure a cheap one, hee hee hee hee." Two things: He talks a lot, and he talks to me; hee hee hee hee. He's on the Trail because Coca-Cola fired him. I can picture his annual review from his supervisor. "Phil is actually a good employee, hard working, smart, and dependable. But his machine-gun giggling is driving me nuts. I woke up in a sweat last night, dreaming of choking him. He is terminated for his own protection." Motor Mouth is not only a fast talker, but also a fast walker and will leave me behind. I intend to slow up even more, hee hee hee hee hee.

I miss Dwayne Drifter, Miz Gorp, Porkchop, Sir Isaac, and even the Doo-Wop Boys. These relationships get close, even over a short period of time. They are only a couple of hundred miles north and probably gone forever. But I am meeting others.

Brown-Skinned Girl is just that. She is the only African-American I have seen on the Trail. She is going to med school, so she has an August deadline. Her boyfriend, *Camel,* carries the water for the two of them. *Recycled* has had a number of new parts installed by his orthopedic surgeon. I later find out he is a judge from Minnesota, trying to thru-hike a second time.

Whisperer is—well—quiet. He had a birthday, but his Trail partner has to tell me that Whisperer turned 20, because I asked Whisperer twice and couldn't hear his response.

Today was good. Great hiking weather, as I enter the Smokies. I am met by a greeter. This is the second time I have met a greeter. The first time was in Laguna, California.

Ah, Laguna. Dana and I have fond memories. When you enter Laguna, there is a little park in the middle of town. A Santa Claus-like man stands there waving his hand, greeting everyone who enters. As I was sitting outside one of its innumerable antique stores where Dana was shopping, Number One walked up to me, the Laguna Greeter. He introduced himself as Number One, and pulled out his California driver's license to prove it. He said he was one of a pair of twins, born as orphans and abandoned at the hospital. He was Number One, his brother was Number Two. He decided to keep his name. He tells me he trades poems for pictures of dead presidents. He recites a poem; I pull out my wallet and give him a picture of a dead president. A simple exchange. Dana returns and the three of us have a long conversation. We liked Number One.

Back to the Smokies. My Smokies greeter is a nice looking man, also similar to Santa, and his job is to tell us the rules of the park. He does it in a nice way, and he greets us in a Number One manner. He smiles and quickly goes down all the rules, which in the Smokies are a bunch, and he wishes you well. I meet a ranger later. He doesn't care to greet me nor wish me well. He just wants to make sure that I hang my bag on the bear pulley.

I am sheltering through a horrific thunderstorm. In spite of the storm now, it was lovely today. I hiked in shorts and one t-shirt. I saw a butterfly with beautiful blue wings and white spots, and pretty little flowers—white, partially purple or all purple spring was evident. But the Smokies won't give up winter easily, and the next few days, according to a Ridge Runner (this is a junior ranger), will be wet and cold.

The Smokies are special. It is the second most visited National Park in the country. There is more "growing stuff" than any other place in the nation. The two things that folks are most interested in are the bears and salamanders. I haven't seen either. The Smokies allow horses, but no dogs. Go figure.

Official people are everywhere. One guy comes by with a little red computer in his hand. It looks like the one Avis has. Attached to a pole that stuck up behind his head, is a white globe, about the size of softball. Sorta Martian-like. "GPS, we're mapping the Trail," he said in a very official way. Official people say things in official ways. Class one: No matter how stupid what you are about to say, say it with authority. He takes my Trail name and scurries off. I feel violated. Why did he and his satellite need to know my Trail name? And why is he mapping the most over-mapped spot on earth? I can see it now.

"Mort, it's official, the switchback above Rocky Top Gap has been erroneously mapped by three feet for all these years. Heads will roll, Mort. Heads will roll!" Pulleeze!

After meeting the greeter, an AT ridge runner, the ranger, and the GPS Nazi—all in one day—I understand why hikers hate the Smokies. Don't even think about throwing your tent down along the Trail, you must stay in shelters with chain-linked fronts—the nastiest shelters on the AT. You stay in the shelters or one of these guys will haul you off to some horrible fate. I think they ship you to Guantanamo.

It's Saturday and the worst day yet. Cold, rainy, no visibility, rocky, slippery. Some hand over hand. I pass Clingmans Dome, the highest point on the AT, and I wouldn't have even known it had it not been for the signs. I hoped for 14 miles this day, I make nine. All my stuff is wet. I hadn't planned to, but it looks like I'll hit Gatlinburg tomorrow and dry out everything and wash off the mud.

E-mail #10–Map Marker #9

Gatlinburg

I am on my way to Gatlinburg, I hope. I pass Mount Collins Shelter—remember we are required to shelter and this was the last shelter before U.S. Highway 441. This means I am committed to make it to the highway before dark and hitch into Gatlinburg. 441 runs through Newfound Gap. I arrive in a horrible fog thinking I would never find a ride. The cars come out of the fog, and pass me before I have a chance to stick out my thumb. But another Trail Angel picks me up. There is a parking lot across the highway; it is a viewpoint for tourists. There is no view, but for some reason my nice angel and his new bride are over there and they honk and offer me a ride. After hiking 18 miles in the rain, I am on my way to Gatlinburg. Everything is either soaked or muddy. Hikers' motels are listed in my trail guide. Those listed—trust me—only hikers should approach. The motel has a little laundromat. I strip right there, totally, and throw everything in the washer and scurry off to my room. I am not hungry—ever. I worry about this; I am losing weight too fast. The klutz factor has kicked in. I slice my finger with my Swiss Army knife and stab myself with my trekking poles. Geometrically impossible, I checked several times, but I did it anyway.

I have left my friend—my walking stick—with Dana, and I am experimenting with trekking poles. These look like ski poles, but with no point on the end; they end concave rather than pointed. The tip is made of something that has purchase even on rocks. Something carbon, I am told, meaning it doesn't slip when you put the point on a rock. A spring is in the shaft to absorb the constant pounding.

The poles really help on the ups. How much up? How much elevation? A thru-hiker ascends 17 times more than an Everest climb. A lot of up. And they are even more support on the downs. I like the poles. They help. I need help. Five million steps. I need help. I miss Dana—it's palpable.

I have been thinking about my answer to question two in chapter one. Why am I doing this? I was too flippant. I'll answer again. It's starting to come to me.

E-mail #11–Map Marker #10

Bryson and I separate.

I wake up in Gatlinburg. April Fools Day 2002. There are a group of hikers waiting for the pancake house to open at 6:00 a.m. Hikers start early. We can't turn on the lights at the end of the day if we are two miles from camp. Particularly when winter hiking, you shouldn't night hike. The number one safety hint is to start early.

I have breakfast with *Gucci* and *Hooch*. They are sixty-ish thru-hikers who say they only plan to do about 10 miles a day. I do the math in my head. " It don't compute." But they are a really cute couple. Gucci is a sharp dresser, therefore his name. Hooch is so nice, so positive. Gucci is a lucky man.

Klutz day is replaced by brain-dead day. I buy a bunch of stuff at the outfitters in Gatlinburg and leave it in the bag on the shuttle. Outfitters almost always have shuttles back to the Trail. And while waiting for the shuttle to return, they sell you stuff. In my case they got to sell this stuff twice. My gloves are also gone. I had them on when I started this morning and they have just evaporated.

I feel totally inept today. How could such a klutz get to Katahdin? Charlie Brown was once told by Lucy, "You, Charlie Brown, you are a real foul ball in the line drive of life. You're in the shadow of your own goal posts. You are a miscue... You are three putts on the eighteenth green... You are a seven-ten split in the tenth frame... A love set! You have dropped a rod and reel in the lake of life... You are a missed free throw, a shanked nine iron and a called third strike." Do you know what Charlie Brown said? "Just wait til next year!" Well, if Charlie Brown can keep on going, so can I.

This is the point that Bill Bryson quit the AT and yellow-blazed. Bill Bryson wrote the famous and funny best seller *A Walk in the Woods*. This was supposedly a story of a thru-hiker, but he finished only about one-tenth of the trail. At this point, he begins to yellow-blaze. White blaze, of course, is following the white blazes on the AT. White marks on trees two inches wide, six inches tall. Alternative trails, not technically on the AT but going the same place, are blue trails. Blue trails sometimes go around mountains rather than straight over them, which is always the case with the AT. They also sometimes go to a pretty overlook, which receives the thru-hikers third finger high sign as we pass. We have little interest in long side trail hikes. Yellow trails are the yellow lines in the middle of the highway, taking a car rather than walking. The highest of no-nos for a thru-hiker. Bryson actually hung it up at Newfound Gap, Highway 441. He started yellow-blazing to finish his book. Too bad, because I have never seen mountain views like those north of Newfound Gap. Fabulous, gorgeous, absolutely breath-taking. The prettiest so far.

Today is a great sunny day, and I am going to the Tri-Corner Knob Shelter. I leave the Park tomorrow. It normally takes three days to hike through the northern half of the Smokies. I choose to do it in two. Tuesday night and Wednesday, the forecast is rain, and I don't want to be caught out again.

I leave the Smokies with mixed feelings. A fabulous piece of land. Misused and obviously under-funded. Sometimes on a ridge you believe you can reach out and touch the next mountain over. I have not had the visual impact like this anywhere else. But the trail is a disaster. Rutted several feet into a groove. The shelters are a national embarrassment. The wonderful spring system is compromised, and too iffy not to purify.

Thru-hikers come through in thousands in March and April, slow months for the Park, which often sees tens of thousands in a day. They herd us together and make us feel so unwelcome that it's at least a massive P.R. disaster.

Sadly, I have to say, I am glad I am through the Smokies. I am never really interested in a return.

Tonight I am bunked at Mountain Moma's, in a tiny bunkhouse outback of a converted schoolhouse. Mountain Moma's sits one mile from the east exit of the Park, called Davenport Gap. Mountain Moma's is famous. It survives by selling cheap North Carolina cigarettes to Tennessee smokers; it sits on the border of the two states. Tobacco being a huge industry in North Carolina, it is not taxed much by the state.

Mountain Moma's also has a grill, a shower, small laundromat (one washing machine, one dryer), bunks for about 20, and a small country store.

It has a hard and unfair reputation of ripping hikers off. Mama does charge you for what you use, but her prices are fair and her hamburgers are to die for. I am in a bunkhouse with six beds, and I use that phrase extraordinarily loosely. Only *Pinetree* and I are in here. There are 8 or 10 other hikers, but they know about Pinetree's snoring. Horrible, loud, no rhythm.

Dispersed explosions of oxygen deprivation. They choose to bunk elsewhere.

I have my airline earplugs. We'll see.

Pinetree is a fabulous person. He started with his grown son at Springer, but his son was fast, and now they are 50 to 100 miles apart. He looks like Wolfman Jack and has a heart of gold. He is always the first to pull something out of his bag to help another hiker. Purification solution, blister medicine, whatever. I think his son is an asshole for leaving him behind. And you know what? In terms of finishing, my money is on Pinetree.

As I mentioned earlier, the Park doesn't allow dogs. There are two other such places on the AT. In New York for 30 miles and Baxter Park in Maine. Around the Smokies, there are entrepreneurs that pick up, board, and deliver your dog to the other side of the park to a dog-friendly site. Mountain Moma's is one such site. Some of my friends had their dogs delivered today. What a reunion! These dogs soon become every hiker's friend.

Pinetree was in the pickup with me that shuttled us back to the AT at the point we left last night. We walked quite a while together. He is a full load. Never stops talking—I want to put him and Maine-ah together. Ali and Frazer all over again.

At the shelters, registers allow hikers to write their thoughts. I see Healed, Sir Isaac, Miz Gorp. I even see an entry from the Flying Porkchop that he was going to town to buy some boots—with better soles. Huh?? With better soles? I hope we are not losing him. But other than these, no one else has appeared lately. Our ranks are depleting.

Stories are everywhere about drop-outs. Blisters, the ups, the cold, the rain, but mostly, their spirits break them down.

Hot Springs is two days ahead. Hot Springs is hiker's heaven. Drop-out hippies built this nice little town in the mountains of North Carolina. It has a real life hot springs spa. I plan to take some time. A zero day? Probably not, but we'll see. It is very cold. Please, please warm up.

Going back, the first day in Cherokee National Forest is somewhat surreal. I started warm—shorts and t-shirt. It got colder—on with the Polartec vest. Cold and spitting later, also foggy—on with the rain suit. So in this fog and rain, I come out of the forest, on to Snowbird Mountain, and suddenly everything was gone—everything. No trees, shrubs, or even grass. This acreage has been scraped to the dirt. In the fog, all I could see was a one-by-four board sticking out of the desolation with an AT blaze; this board directed our type through that scorched or scraped earth. It was beyond surreal, a twilight zone picture. When I arrive at Groundhog Creek Shelter seconds before the hardest rain, I ask around. No one knew what had been done to the top of that mountain. I still don't know.

When I arrive, the shelter is full. But *Ballou*, who will require his own chapter, scoots over and makes room. We are shoulder-to-shoulder. I have the last possible space. *Helen* and *Giggles*, the Canadian girls, show up later. All of us, being perfect gentlemen, pointed down stream to a nice spot for the two of them to tent up. (Sorry girls.)

Ballou and Dan are talking about sticking a chicken up a cow's butt at the time I go to sleep.

E-mail #12–Map Marker #11

Max Patch is a Wonderland.

Max cleared his acreage for sheep and cattle. His acreage was on the top of a mountain. This acreage now resides in the Cherokee Forest. The land has changed hands through the years, and is now owned by the Forest Service for the use of the AT. We walked up the mountain for hours to get to the top of this meadow in the middle of the wilderness. Amazing to spin 360 degrees, no trees, and a perfect view of the mountains in any direction. Because of the warmth of the South, the tree line always exceeds the highest mountains. Max Patch offers us one of the few unimpeded views. Max Patch is a wonderland.

The forest is coming alive. Greens, purples, violets are starting to show up along with the grays and browns we are so used to. The naked trees, which have not quite budded, make the views easier, but I will be thankful for the canopy of green.

Bernie tells us his five-year-old knee replacement is giving out. I meet Bernie one day south of Hot Springs. I don't expect to see him after Hot Springs. Bernie misses his grandchildren from his three children and eight foster children. I am not sure if Bernie really has a bad knee or a lonely knee. He probably wants some grandchildren on it.

Please warm up, please, please.

All of a sudden I have a blister problem. A serious one. I'll work through it.

E-mail #13–Map Marker #12

Hot Springs—Just right

Hot Springs, North Carolina, is one of those places whose time is now. In ten years, it will be discovered. The little strip hotels will have shut down, the $2.00 beers at Paddlers Pub will be history, the friendly comfortable pop culture will be lost. The two hardware stores will be selling trendy antiques, and the spa will be $200 a day.

But for now, it is perfect. It is a hiker's heaven.

Just right. Everything close, just as close as we all become these two days. The outfitter has everything you need: great free coffee and helpful, experienced hikers for sales people. Three affordable restaurants within 100 feet. The spa has a mineral bath and a massage for $50. It will be discovered soon, and it will be taken from the hikers. My guess is when that happens, the AT will be relocated. But for now, it runs right through the middle of Main Street. When you enter with your 40-pound pack and your beard, everything about Hot Springs says, "here I am thru-hiker, stay with me awhile."

The bluegrass band is authentic. Men and women from the mountains, respecting the music from generations ago. Nothing electric, nothing amplified.

Hot Springs is perfect. I leave reluctantly.

I take a zero. Mostly because Dana drove up, but also to rest my blisters. A day where you have progressed zero miles towards Maine is called a zero. You have laid-out. You rested. Many thru-hikers say they will take no zeros, they will eventually break down, and many take a zero every week or two weeks. I plan to take between 10–15 zeros, not counting one special meeting with the University of Georgia.

E-mail #14

The blisters

I am still fighting blisters. They can pull you off the trail. Right may be better; left, I fear is worse. Left is now a hole behind my Achilles, just above my heel. The hole is about the size of a quarter. The blister has long since left. The hole is a complete loss of skin down to a red membrane.

To touch it in any way kills. Sock, boot, tape, in any way. When you walk up hill, your foot slides back in your boot and pushes against the heel. The pain is excruciating. My body is getting in shape, and can handle the ups, but now my feet are the problem.

I will try a new combination of tape tomorrow. It is expected to be warmer tomorrow. Thank you, thank you for that.

E-mail #15

Something simpler

Two days of rain on and off. Overcast, dark, gray. On days like this there are no views. The hike is all work, and no joy. I just try to keep dry.

Maybe the bad blister on the left is a bit better today. Maybe.

I am eating better. I am still not hungry, but my body is accepting food, and I am pushing it down. I weigh about 205 pounds. That's about 15–20 pounds lighter than the last time any of my family or friends saw me. I burn about 6,000 calories a day, impossible to offset on the Trail, so I eat a lot when I go to town. Ever want to eat all you can? As often as you want? Anything you want? Especially junk food? Lots and lots of sugar? Become a thru-hiker.

I think when I hike. Family, business, and things more esoteric. Love, spirituality, consideration, poetry and colors.

I sing or hum on the Trail. Songs with a good hiking beat. I also think. The Trail makes you think, and lets you think. It unravels complicated thoughts into something much simpler. For many, and I meet more of them every day, the Trail is their religion. It is the connection to their spiritual need. It finds, for them, peace.

E-mail #16–Map Marker #13

My Trail Angel

Pinetree, as I have mentioned, has been the general store on the Trail. You have a need, Pinetree will solve it. He has become not only the general store, but also the cabaret. He is carrying, in addition to his already overabundant pack, a full-size guitar and a collection of harmonicas. The heaviest are the harmonicas. Pinetree, I guess, expects to entertain us all the way to Maine. Astonishing. Each day on the Trail is grueling and hard. Carrying all that stuff makes Pinetree's day a living hell. And once the day is over, food and sleep are all we care about.

Music around the campfire? In most forests, we cannot have fires. But most importantly, no one wants music.

And if Pinetree starts singing, as much as I love him, I will personally switch his channel.

My blisters are past the point of self-doctoring. Right seems well, but left is bad. Also, my left Achilles tendon doesn't work well. I can't play around any longer, I am going to hitch in to Erwin and get a doctor's advice.

Somehow through the pain, I climb and finally stand on Big Bald. And I am totally alone. It is spiritual. This huge mountain 5,500 feet up, topped in meadow, is more awesome than Max Patch by its sheer magnitude. Where is everyone? No one at all, I am totally alone. I enjoy this very much; I enjoy the solitude.

An hour or so after descending, a fast hiker catches up with me and says that Pinetree has hitched back to Hot Springs to mail his cabaret equipment home. Why back to Hot Springs? Why not forward to Erwin? Watch out Pinetree, you'll get sucked in.

It's over. I can't take another step. The pain brings water to my eyes. I try to walk up on my toes so no part of my boot touches the back half of my foot. This doesn't work very far. Worse yet, my Achilles has finally blown out, from trying to hike on my toes, I think. My trail *Data Book* tells me a mostly deserted road is ahead. To my surprise, it is paved, but it is truly deserted. I stand there for a good ten minutes. Then I think I can hear a car coming. Not a car, a pickup. I don't stick out my thumb, standing in the middle of the road I wave my arms. Getting run down would be an OK result right now. The driver stops and I walk around to talk through the open window. This man has a hundred good reasons to drive off. I don't know what expression I had on my face, but it must have been pitiful. All I can remember saying is I had to get to a doctor, and we were on our way to Erwin. When we arrive at the clinic twenty minutes later my angel would accept no payment. He waits around to see how I am doing. Finally, he tells me he has to get back to his church. He teaches Sunday school and Wednesday is prayer meeting night. He had been on his way there when he picked me up. He calls his class from the hospital pay phone and asks them to wait, and as soon as he is sure I am all right, he gets back in his truck and continues on his hour detour to church, which turns out to be only a mile from where he picked me up. He must now turn around and drive all the way back there.

This is the first of three unsolicited kindnesses I received these few days.

Erwin, Tennessee is a major hiking center and most of this culture is centered around two hostels. Uncle Johnnie's and Miss Janet's. These two people hate each other, and the competition is fierce. The competition is a good thing for the hikers, because the two of them offer lots of services hard to find on most of the trail. They shuttle, arrange slack-packing, give rides to restaurants, and have good prices.

Erwin is also known as the town that hanged an elephant. The less said about that, the better.

Good news. The doc thinks I only need to take a day or two off and he gives me a lot of good help on how to treat my blisters. And my Achilles is fine.

I bunk in with Carol and Jeff Clayton at their bed & breakfast. They shouldn't let a muddy, smelly hiker into their B&B, but they do. I choose this rather than either of the hostels because it is almost next to the hospital, and I simply can't walk any farther. I become family immediately. Great folks. They take me in despite their no-hikers rule.

They are from Buffalo, New York. Stopped into Erwin one day, and never left.

I am stuck with another zero, unplanned. That's okay. Particularly if I take one, walking will stop hurting. They are the second trail angels to surface during my foot saga.

E-mail #17

Ichabod Crane

Overnight, I make a compromise with my doctor. (However, my doctor is not aware of it). I will go back to where I hitched in to the clinic, 11 miles from Erwin, and I will slack-pack in. I call Uncle Johnnie for a shuttle. Only 11 miles, no pack, an easy day, but not a zero. I am told this is a very easy 11 miles and I can do it in some cheap sneakers I bought, which I altered to accommodate the blister pattern.

The day goes fine; my blisters looked better. The real secret is duct tape. After I put all the first aid on my feet including tape, the doc said wrap it all in duct tape, it will keep the other tape from sliding around when I sweat. It worked! Tomorrow, Uncle Johnnie will shuttle me 19 miles north of Erwin, and I will slack-pack back. One more test of these wimpy feet.

I have been lucky with views. After Blye Gap, at the North Carolina border, there are four potential great views. Clingmans Dome, Max Patch, Big Bald, and Beauty Spot. Clingmans Dome is the highest point on the AT at 6,800 feet. It was socked in, and if I wore a watch, I could not have read it. But Big Bald and Max Patch were beautiful clear days, and the views were fabulous. You just had to sit down in the meadow and drink those views in. Wonderful.

Today I reach the Beauty Spot, and it is clear enough to appreciate. I enjoy a banana sandwich with one of my friends on Beauty Spot. (Because I am hiking south this section, I run into a lot of folks I know). So the big time views get two A's, two B's and an F.

My 19-mile test might have been a bit much on my foot, but it seems okay. The day finishes directly in front of Uncle Johnnie's. He runs me up the hill to the B&B.

Johnnie tells me this almost unbelievable story. Something that happened at his hostel today. There was this guy working on his laptop computer on the front porch. A guy named *Del Doc*. A doctor from Delaware, a former thru-hiker. Anyway, there he is on Johnnie's front porch. Johnnie's helper is cutting the grass. He runs over the extension cord Del Doc has used to plug in his computer. *Pop!* It says. Del Doc has lost all his data and begins to go a little crazy and throws a metallic white ball he has at the helper. White ball? It's the GPS Nazi! The little officious asshole from the Smokies! He has lost all his data! Del Doc is the Map Nazi and he lost all his data! There is a God.

Jeff and Carol are setting dinner. Special, they said. They like to celebrate Friday nights, and I am invited.

Carol tells me all about her two nephews who needed rescuing. Their mother, Carol's sister, had a devastating car accident and lost half of her brain. Carol—single—stepped up. She then discovered she couldn't pull this off by herself. She confronted her boyfriend, Jeff, about her need for help. "Marry me and help me raise the boys." He went off to think about it. Raising two young men was more than he had bargained for. He came back two days later, held Carol's hand, and said two words. "I'm in."

They marry, adopt the two boys, and raise them as their own. The two boys turned out fine. They are grown and on with their own lives. Decades later Jeff and Carol are starting life again as they had expected to long ago—just the two of them. Very much in love, starting over in Erwin, Tennessee, with the Clayton Dogwood Inn, their bed & breakfast. They like their life and it rubs off.

I leave them reluctantly tomorrow, heading north.

Today, I top Unaka Mountain, 5,200 feet. Spooky. All of a sudden, heavy fog surrounds me. I am hiking alone, as usual. What I don't know is that this mountain was wiped out many decades ago by a forest fire. The next several years, the weather favored the red spruce, and this tree took over the top of Unaka. All the trees seem identical, and they create a dense, dark canopy, under which I am walking in the fog. This scene is truly out of Ichabod Crane. I can't see the trail; right and left seem identical; my only hope to get out of this spot will be the white blazes on the trees that represent the AT.

I get lost twice. I keep telling myself "I am on top of a mountain, if I get lost, just go down. Don't get rattled." But I have to tell you how happy I am to have these blazes lead me out of this red spruce forest.

Roane Mountain is ahead, and very hard hiking will be a daily occurrence until I get close to Damascus. This stretch in Tennessee is short but intense. Roane is the last mountain above 6,000 feet that I will experience until I reach the Whites, the Whites, the Whites.

E-mail #19

The dragon lives.

Thru-hikers fear the dragon.

The beast that slays their dream of a thru-hike. Blisters are not a dragon. They can delay you, but unless they get infected, they won't stop you. All of us have our dragons. Lewis the *Lone Ranger* (who always hikes in a group) fears his diabetes. He must keep it regulated. *Ballou*, I am concerned, may have Giardia. And his main concern is not what Giardia can do to him, but the cancellation of his thru-hike.

I had two potential dragons when I started. My back, which was my number one worry, is cooperating. I think my back likes the Trail, and doesn't want to mess things up. My left knee gets shot by a dart every so often. I am walking the Trail, and the pain freezes me in my tracks. Some sumbitch has shot me in the knee with a dart gun. Or at least it feels like it. I cannot figure out what I did or what type of step I took that caused this short burst of agony. But if the knee goes...

E-mail #18–Map Marker #14

Roane Mountain

Roane Mountain is the hardest 10 miles I have had so far. Up—steep—very steep—more up—slip back—the pack weighs 300 pounds (doesn't it?). I keep forcing candy down. More sugar, more energy. Hours, and hours, and hours of up.

I do make it and my blisters look and feel no worse.

Roane once had a hotel, the famous Cloudland Hotel. The ballroom was split by the Tennessee/North Carolina state line. One state was dry, the other wet. Carrying your drink across the state line could land you in the pokey. The concrete foundation is all that survives. As do the spirit and memories of the hotel, I hope.

The shelter here, High Roane, is the highest on the Appalachian Trail. 6,300 feet. It was the former fire warden's cabin. Big and roomy as shelters go. The area is dominated by rhododendrons. Supposedly a very rare rhododendron, the Catawba, is still present here. Come in June—they say—and the smells are beyond belief—they say. I am a little tired of hearing about how I "just missed" something fabulous or something that is soon coming up.

The 33 miles between Roane and Dennis Cove is supposedly hell. There is no way to do it except 13 and 20. It will be my first 20. I hate the thought.

The 20-mile section is tough. But as always, there are memories. I am high on this summit above a morning fog. I can see the tops of mountains across from me, but below, about half way down, a carpet of swirling fog stretched from that mountain to mine. I can see the carpet rise. It reaches me, and what was once fog below slowly becomes clouds above, and the valley emerges to my view. Magical.

—Roan High Knob Shelter. Was built as the fire rangers cabin.

E-mail #20

Damascus

This is an entry I thought I might never write. I told Dana I would not write it until I reached Damascus. Why I picked Damascus, I am not sure, but I do know I couldn't face it at the time. By the same token, I feel I couldn't avoid it forever.

If I care about all of you, it must be written. It is and was a major event of the journey. If I am going to write a journal of the journey, it cannot be excluded. But I hate the writing of each word. Mostly I hate it because to do this, means to relive it. But also because I am afraid I will write it poorly, and you will think me silly. But like the Trail, it must be dealt with in order for us to move on.

Let's go back to Map Marker 4; it ends with "a hard day ends well." Well it didn't. Sadly, it didn't end well at all.

After checking into the motel, I called Dana to let her know that I had moteled up.

Remember, back in February, I was still in Georgia only two hours from home.
Dana said the words I secretly hoped she would, "I'm coming up to see you."
A couple of hours later, the knock came, and in came my two favorites. Dana and Tallulah.

Tallulah was our Havanese dog. You remember her; she was with Dana and me the day I started. Two years old. I have always had a dog, all shapes, breeds, and colors. But Tallulah was unique. I've spent a lot of time trying to figure out why. Both Dana and I clearly would say she is our favorite pet of all the ones we had owned.

I have heard people say, who have children with disabilities, that their affection for them is magnified. That they felt a special love to protect and nurture. Maybe this was part of it. You see, Tallulah was mostly deaf. But gosh, how we loved that little dog!

Because she couldn't hear, she would have to look at you to gain an understanding of what you wanted. Because of this, Tallulah had eye contact. She seemed to hang on your words, even though she couldn't hear them.

When she took a nap, she would slip one paw onto your leg, that way you couldn't get up without her knowing about it. She would rest in a high, strategic place, where she could see what was going on. The back of the sofa was her favorite.

You couldn't even think about going somewhere without her knowing about it, almost at the moment you decided to go.

She was easy to take places. Everyone was happy to see her. She was immensely popular at the University of Georgia in Athens, and loved to run in circles at Herty Field when we went for our evening walk.

Lisa, my sister-in-law and illustrator for this book, was an important part of Tallulah's life. Theirs was a huge, mutual affection. And Lisa would sometimes come over and pick Tallulah up "to spend the night." She particularly liked to have Tallulah when David was out of town. Dana would gather Tallulah's stuff in her little overnight bag. Seeing this, Tallulah would know that she was going to visit Lisa. A normally quiet animal would yelp, she knew she was going to see Virginia, their lab who adored her, but it was really Lisa that she was excited to see.

Tallulah was considerate. Never over-affectionate. Just right.

She would win over the nastiest personalities. Our cat, Sapelo, among them. The two of them played endlessly, rolling around together as one ball. Then exhausted they would curl up and sleep, impossible to tell where one ended and the other began. On the inside of our car windows, Tallulah has left nose tracks where she looked with great interest at the world outside.

She could hear high pitches. The beep the security system triggered when cars entered our driveway would send her to the kitchen window to welcome whoever was coming.

I can tell you, the last year brought me home in as low spirits as I have ever known. To see her at that window, wanting nothing in life but to greet me, was a gift none but she could bestow.

She also had a secret life of friends. Virgil, our mentally handicapped neighbor, came under her spell. Whenever she could, she would sneak away through the backyard and visit.

So there they were. My two favorites. Dana and I went to dinner, leaving Tallulah in the motel room.

We returned to the room, finding the door cracked open. It had not closed fully when we left two hours ago. It was freezing, we were in a strange town, it was late, the motel was on a large, busy road, and Tallulah was out. And surely terrified and lost.

Dana got in the car. I stayed on foot. I whistled; Dana clapped. We rushed to every adjoining establishment and asked about Tallulah.

The town was mostly deserted—a tourist town in February. But a few convenience stores were open and gas stations. I flagged down a policeman I saw. He called his colleague, and the two of them truly tried to help. Driving back and forth in front and behind closed businesses. I had a sense of dread. She couldn't hear, she was lost, it was bitterly cold, and the wind was blowing unmercifully.

Then one of the policemen drove up quickly. He had seen her behind a building. We took off. Dana in the car, me on foot.

Tallulah wasn't there, or at least we couldn't find her.

I went northward, Dana cruised southward. We were at least three blocks apart, but I could see Dana's car barely. Then it stopped. The door opened, I thought, then it drove on jerky, I thought, something was happening. I turned and ran. Then I heard it. It was a pleading moan, high, piercing, again and again. It was Dana.

The dread sank deep in my stomach. I continued to run. When I came upon the car, it stood in the middle of the street, as did Dana, holding a lifeless Tallulah.

Dana only stopped this rending moan to take a breath. Then again. I can now tell, it is the word "no" almost as a question. I came up to the two of them and held them.

Later, Dana told me the most touching and tragic part of this saga. She had actually found Tallulah alive, running across a gas station lot. She got out and called her only fifteen yards away. She does this by clapping; it is something Tallulah can hear. Tallulah stopped and looked at her.

Whatever was going on in her little mind, whatever combination of emotions were happening, we'll never know. Could she not see Dana in the car lights? Dana was in our son Brett's car. Did she not recognize it? The wind, the cold, the strangeness of the place. She was surely frantic.

But for whatever reason, Tallulah, rather than running to the one she loved most, as she had always done a thousand times before, ran the other way.

Straight into the highway.

Dana was completely inconsolable, devastated.

We came home from Helen. We cared for our friend and companion, and moved on. But we moved on with a vacuum in our daily routine. When we recognized the reason, it brought great sadness crushing down.

Four weeks before Tallulah died, her older sister became a grandmother four times in a beautiful litter in Birmingham, Alabama. Just before I reached Damascus, Dana met a little girl in this litter, and picked her out before she received her papers. When they came, Dana discovered that this puppy was Tallulah's grandniece. Earlier, Dana had insisted I return to the Trail, and I was on Sassafras Mountain when Dana found this puppy and made her the most recent member of our family.

Sassafras is home now, is winning Sapelo over, and is filling Dana's heart with love.

We scattered Tallulah's ashes on the little path where she ran to bring sunshine to Virgil's day.

We hugged, and I put Tallulah's dog tags on my walking stick. And like the Trail, life does go on, but there is a spot back there that belongs only to her. Fine and faithful friend—Tallulah.

E-mail #21–Map Marker #15

One million footprints

Dana is coming to Damascus, and I can't wait. Happy birthday to all my April special people. I can remember I was always busy in March and April thinking of stuff for all of you, and buying birthday presents. Maybe next year, I'll double up (maybe not).

Today, I did a relatively easy 13 miles and went by the exquisite Laurel Falls. Waterfalls are somewhat common on the Trail, but Laurel Falls is particularly beautiful. Very hard to get to, but worth it. More like rock climbing than hiking.

Damascus, Virginia, is a defining moment on the AT.

I have left Georgia, North Carolina, and Tennessee.

I have finished over 450 miles.

I have left a million footprints.

I have camped, sheltered, and hiked in the foulest of weather, never missing a day.

Of all my colleagues who started at Springer Mountain, only 25 percent remain.

This adventure is quite real now.

I now know I will do this. If the dragon leaves me alone, and my friends and family remain steadfast—I will do this.

E-mail #22

The rules

The only memento hikers receive when they complete their thru-hike is a 2,000-Mile Badge they sew on their back pack. The AT is 2,168 (this year), but to begin with decades ago, it was approximately 2,000 miles. The badge hasn't changed. The rule to receive a 2000-Mile Badge is walk the Trail until it is completed—that's pretty much it.

North to south is okay. South to north is okay. Some south, some north, that's okay.

Full pack, half a pack, no pack is okay.

Leave some harder white blazes for easier blue blazes, that's okay if there was a good reason for doing so. For example, I took a blue blaze around a mountain top when the mountain top was on fire.

In short, the ATC doesn't want to get into the rulebook business. They want to encourage hikers to the Trail, and they insist that this rule thing is to be self-administered, on the honor system.

Most of us stumble and bumble our way forward. We get on the wrong trail from time to time, we get lost in town, we get lost period, but we find our way back and continue on.

I hear there are purists. They feel that if you get lost, you must go back to the exact spot that you got lost, and continue the AT from that point. If you enter a shelter from a south access path, you must not leave the next morning on the north access path; rather you must go back south and pick up the AT from there. I have not met one of these guys yet, but I can't wait. We all know we will walk a couple of hundred miles more than the AT's 2,168 miles. We have tons of hiking miles in the bank.

I have yet to see a hiker abuse the spirit of thru-hiking. The ATC is smart to stay out of it.

I think I'll drop a few pet rocks in the pack of the first purist I meet. They would seem to be the type of people who would be happy to lug a pet rock a few miles. As Motor Mouth would say ... hee, hee, hee, hee, hee.

E-mail #23

More characters

Tim doesn't have a Trail name—just Tim. He calls his wife every night he can, and they meet somewhere on the Trail every 10 days or so. She drives from Ohio.

Tim weighs 215 pounds today. A year ago, he weighed almost 100 pounds more. He quit his real job and now makes fine furniture by hand—the style is Amish, although he isn't. This year he is a thru-hiker. His weight is down as is his blood pressure. In a very real way, the Trail is saving his life.

Stone and *Sly* are cool. That's all there is to it. Stone is 20, handsome, blonde, tall and thin. A face that turns lights on. What a smile. Sly is two and a half. He and I share hamburgers and peanuts. Sly likes me a lot, but his first love is Stone. Stone picked him out of a filthy pen at the Humane Society, and that was that, for life.

Sly went over a cliff after some deer yesterday, but he crawled back up after much howling and barking, no worse for the experience.

Turkey Bacon cannot be liked. I try and I try, but he does everything wrong. Says everything wrong. Well, not everything. After 400 miles, he told me my sleeping bag was inside out. And it was.

Red Hat returned. Red Hat's stuff is all red. His pack, his shirt, his hat, his gaiters, his pack cover. You can see him coming for a mile. He is wonderful, but he is not pretty. His skin is also red, and his hair would be red if he had any.

He hung out with me all day today. We talked as we walked. He is completely lost. Not in the woods, but in life. No telling what's going to happen to him when he quits the Trail. He is 22, a college flunk-out, but very smart. He is engaging and everyone likes him. But he is lost.

He kept looking to me for an answer. I have become this group's Gramps. I am 56;

most of them are in their twenties. They are so adventurous, so poised, so confident, but all of a sudden, like a window shade snapping open, revealing that they are very young again. Even afraid. And they are looking to me. I have all my wise advice ready.

"Call her tonight."

"Don't decide that now, you have plenty of time."

"The Trail will still be here when you come back. Go home."

I have said all these things and more, but I don't know what to say to Red Hat.

He is unique. A free spirit. One day he got up, packed all his gear, and started up the Trail. He walked only three miles, unpacked all of his stuff, put up his tent in the middle of the Trail—crawled in and prepared to go to sleep. As I walked by, I heard him say, "Short day today, Bearfoot."

Red Hat disappeared. I happen to know he has a girlfriend in Boone, North Carolina. He has been gone about four days.

Today, Sly and Stone and *Jeff*, a really cool section hiker, were with me crossing a gravel road. Literally from the bushes, Red Hat sticks out his head. "Hey!" he said. We all burst out laughing. He was gone. Now he has returned. We won't get finicky about the 40 miles he missed during his detour to Boone. We are just glad he is back. Red Hat has returned.

E-mail #24

A true story from the past

Richie Rich had all the latest gear. The best backpack, boots, gear galore. When he grew tired of something, he would drop it in the Hiker Box. The Hiker Box is free stuff to any hiker who finds it. And Richie dropped some damn fine stuff in the Hiker Box.

If a hiker was low on cash, Richie would give him $20. Not a loan. Great guy Richie.

Richie disappeared. He left his pack and everything. He left a note letting it be known that he would be back in a week or two. Hikers guarded his stuff. No one was going to mess with Richie's gear.

He never came back. He returned to California to rob a bank. This was his occupation, and the FBI gave him a long, imposed detour.

I often wonder who I am camping next to.

E-mail #25

Red Hat quit. He went home. I will miss him. I will really miss him. And I also feel I let him down.

E-mail #26

More Damascus

Damascus is the second greatest hiking town that we have seen so far. Only second to Hot Springs. Trail Days are held in Damascus. Hikers have their own convention in Damascus. Tents everywhere. 10,000 hikers camp out in the parks, vacant lots, church lawns, everywhere. Massive quantities of beer are consumed. The whiff of other intoxicants is in the air. Bands, contests, on and on.

The AT comes through town, and trails with all kinds of great names spider through the mountains. Hikers like Damascus.

But bicycling is even bigger. Damascus welcomes hundreds of thousands of these folks each year. Why? The Virginia Creeper.

In the 1800s, a buddy of Robert E. Lee's came to this valley and named the town Damascus after a city in Syria. Don't know why.

There was iron ore that had to be pulled out.

A narrow gauge railroad was started, and almost finished, but cheaper and better ore was found elsewhere. So there you go. Then a fellow connected to the Roosevelts—I think he married one—bought all the good forestland for 50 cents an acre. He needed this railroad to be finished, and it was.

Soon the rape of the land began.

The railroad was slow because narrow gauge would derail otherwise. Though slow, it could pull the wood out. And it did. It also hauled passengers, particularly on the weekends. They were more impatient than the wood, and would constantly try to convince the engineer to go faster. When he did, the Creeper would derail, and they would spend their Sunday putting it back on its tracks. Because of its speed, or lack of, the rail line was named the Virginia Creeper. You know, like the Orient Express. Same kind of thing.

One of the sad stories told to me by an old-timer was about the chestnut trees. They were cut down in 5-foot sections, and hauled out by the Creeper. Then they were boiled for their oil and discarded.

The chestnut was certainly the most magnificent tree ever to grace North America. Fabulous. Huge. It dwarfed the largest live oak. Now it is virtually extinct. Fine furniture and grainy black and white pictures taken in the 20s, or before, is all that's left. Like the chestnut tree, the Creeper almost became extinct. The wood was gone and once-loyal passengers bought cars. Passenger service stopped in the 60s, freight service in the 70s. The Creeper's main engine sits in a park in Damascus. quiet now, still. The railroad line ran through mountain and river property you can only dream about.

Rails to Trails.

Private and federal funds turned this right-of-way over to the people of Southwest Virginia. And, you know, they done good.

You can rent a bike, get shuttled 17 miles up into the mountains, and coast downhill all the way back to Damascus through forests, little villages, over 20 or 30 bridges, past fly fishermen, beside waterfalls, and generally experience the best of what is outside.

If you have the energy, because it is not downhill any more, you can start pedaling and pedal all the way to Abington, 14 miles farther.

Our young forests are fighting back. The trees are adolescents, but they are gaining maturity. This is the case for all the AT. The entire Eastern wilderness is recovering from early last century logging. If you find a mature tree, it's probably an accident. There are few old-growth forests left in the East.

In Georgia, for example, logging was so big, that the tiny port of Darien was the second largest seaport in the world during logging's peak. Massive pines, almost impossible to find today, were clear-cut for an unbroken century.

But this is a new century, and the children walking the Creeper today only know that the trees seem plenty big to them and the Trail is a place where families have fun.

Dana and I have the Creeper to ourselves. It is Monday, and a cool April day, the 22nd—her birthday. It is a little early for tourists, but perfect for us. We rent bikes and coast down the Creeper. Tomorrow she drops me off at the Trail, and we go about this AT adventure some more.

E-mail #27–Map Marker #17

I love Virginia.

I am 90 miles into Virginia, and I understand why many hikers choose this state as their favorite.

Mainly, it has variety. Mountains, meadows, streams, small villages, and ridge walking. Let's talk a bit about ridge walking. The farmers choose the bottomland. The mountains that rise between the farmland were left pretty much untouched. The backbone of these mountains is the ridges that run southwest to northeast for hundreds of miles. The AT runs along the top of these ridges. Pretty. Genteel.

We see much more of Virginia than any other state. More than 500 miles. So it's good that we like it.

Virginia has one contest won easily so far—the best breakfast in the world. Miz Jenny at the Lazy Fox in Damascus cannot, and will not, be beat. Too many superlatives. Miz Jenny says she is second to Keith Shaw at Shaw's in Monsoon, Maine. I will withhold my opinion for 1,500 miles and see for myself.

I am afraid to write this, but my blisters are better. It is clear when you are my age that doing something like this it really comes down to pain management. Something hurts all the time.

E-mail #28

Thru-hikers all hate PUDs.

As I told you, the Trail is maintained by a bunch of trail clubs. It is instantaneously recognizable when you move from one club to the next. Different signage, different attitude about clearing the trail, blow-downs particularly, but most importantly, where the Trail goes.

The Trail is constantly being relocated, often for good reasons. But also because these trail clubs lose it. They think their little 50 miles should be a survival test, a macho competition to be the hardest 50 miles on the AT. They run the AT back and forth across streams, they seek out a rock outcropping and push the AT through it; but worse, the Pointless Up and Down (PUD). Every wannabe mountain has a little bump on top.

If these trail clubs don't respect the AT, don't understand the vision, don't respect the hiker, they will run the Trail over every PUD in their kingdom. We hate them. Sure it's hard, but every day is hard. We are angry because it is pointless.

Every hiker hates PUDs and the PUD makers.

E-mail #29–Map Marker #18

April 30, 2002

22 miles to Pearisburg. Too long for one day, too short for two.

I decide to leave early because I'll be covering 22 miles today. I am at the trailhead at 5:30.

There is a national forest register at the Trail Head. I am the first to sign. I am definitely the first, and about 100 spider webs prove it.

22 hard miles, lots of rocks. Bruised feet for sure. Beat up knees, and for some reason, I'm dragging. You should not go into the rocks dragging. "Pick up your feet," Stone would say. "Bearfoot, you're going to break your ankle, pick up your feet." Stone's not here though. I'm all alone.

The foliage is filling out and I can no longer "look through" the forest. I am surrounded by the here and now.

For 11 grueling hours, I see not one person.

But I see wildlife. I'm always being asked about wildlife, and I have no stories except, uh, squirrels. Pretty lame. But today is different. Today, I see wildlife.

In the first hour, a large deer leaps across the Trail, not 10 yards away. He stops, notices me, and backtracks across the Trail. He slows down, but then he turns it on. Tail skyward, he turns on the jets. Wow!

After missing this picture, I relocate my little camera into my back pocket. You know, for the quick draw. I will nail Bambi next time.

Hours of joyless hiking, concentrating on every step. Rocks suck. Shins, ankles, and feet really hurt. Trekking poles clicking and working hard. Their carbon tips stick to the stones; these poles are invaluable. I would have fallen at least twice without them. Falling in a rock bed is not pretty.

You can't look up or you're dead meat, you will fall. So because my head is down, what I saw today was doubly miraculous.

The Trail is normal for a few yards. Ground not rocks. I hear a screech. The largest owl I have ever seen flies over and lands in a dead tree directly over my head. I am captivated. He checks me out. Unimpressed, he takes off.

Oops! My camera remains in my back pocket. I don't think I would have lasted very long in old Dodge City.

I have completed 10 of my 22 miles. I check my *Data Book* and do a little mental calculating. I don't want to be hiking in the dark. It will be close. I try to speed up my battered legs a bit.

On the Trail you spot things ahead. Often, almost always, it is a fallen log that takes on all kinds of shapes. Like bears. I spotted 100 bears that turned out to be a twisted log.

But this one moves.

I freeze and look closely, and we are looking at each other. He—I guess—is stretching high to get a better look at me.

He is a black bear as all East Coast bears are, but he isn't black. Light brown, almost blonde. This means he is a cub.

His mom must be around so I don't walk toward him, as much as I want to. Camera out, I drop it. Shit. I pick it up. He is still there. Click. Probably from too far away, but I get it. He is giving me his profile, and I stand there as long as I can, and scan the area for mom. Then I move on up the Trail. One last look.

Just to punctuate the day, later I see a billy goat. Whiskers, a bell around his neck, he is standing in the Trail. He is up 3,500 feet from whoever gave him that bell and at least three miles away. It is obviously his Trail, he will not move. And he turns toward me in a way I am not enamored with. I bushwhack around him carefully, and head down the mountain slightly ahead of sunset. 22 miles, a deer, an owl, a bear cub, and a goat. A great way to close April, I think to myself. Also closing 650 miles. Not only miles, but also some memories forever engraved.

In Pearisburg, I run into Stone and Jeff, our section-hiker friend. We have dinner and much beer.

We talk about the murder that occurred on the section we just finished. It was about 15 years ago and, what seems to always be the case, it wasn't hiker-on-hiker violence. A drugged-out factory worker, Randall Lee Smith, drove to a campsite and then walked farther up into the Jefferson National Forest to the AT. He murdered a couple in the Wapiti II Shelter and tried to bury them. Bob Mountford and Susan Ramsay were social workers from Maine. Hugely popular hikers, they were known for their generosity and good humor. Smith shot Mountford in his sleep. Then, with much violence, knifed Susan Ramsay again and again. He was captured at a nearby beach resort. There is almost no violence on the AT. It is much safer than walking on a city street. But all the books warn hikers to be especially careful when they are close to a road crossing. I now realize why there was a forest service register entering this section. When the couple became missing, they were difficult to locate because no one knew just how far they had progressed. The registers are a way of keeping up with hikers. That is why as we pass shelters, we make entries even though we don't plan to stay. There are registers in every shelter and at entrances to most parks. The couple crossed Dismal Creek to reach an area where they died. It was called Angels Rest. I hope so.

E-mail #30

Where to sleep

Thanks for all your voice mails. One of your questions is about sleeping. There are a number of options.

1. Under the stars. Throw your ground cloth down, put your sleeping mat over it, and your sleeping bag over the mat. A fine option in good weather.

> No matter what your place in life
> Or your state of mind
> Having a star-packed sky
> Be part of your night
> Made you rich
> —Toni Morrison

2. The next level is a tarp. We all carry a lightweight, synthetic tarp. Attach a line between two trees, drape the tarp over it, and tack it to the ground with tent stakes. Now you have a little protection from the rain, although not the bugs.

3. Hundreds of shelters, also called lean-tos, have been constructed on, or near, the AT by the AT hiking clubs. No electricity. No water. Maybe a privy nearby. You sleep on a wooden floor with whoever shows up; you share this space with mice, snakes, and lots of bugs. You hang your food sack on suspended ropes away from the shelter to keep the bears from visiting in the middle of the night. Claim a sliver of wooden floor, and follow the "under the stars" procedure. All your stuff is under roof now, and will be dry if bad weather comes. The hard wooden surface, snoring, and mice are the negatives. Your backpack will hang from a length of rope some former hiker left for you. There is a knot in the rope with a can (often tuna) with a hole in its bottom and the rope threaded through the hole. The can dangles about half way down. This keeps the varmints from crawling down the rope and into your pack. Mice, rats, squirrels, even snakes. On the end of the rope a stick about four inches long is tied. This is what

— A typical shelter, also called a lean-to,

— My first walking stick is leaning on the roof

— There are hundreds of these shelters along the trail, this one is a nice one —

you hang your pack loop from.

Mice? Sure, and a lot of them. All food is supposedly eaten away from the shelter—but ... mice get active at night. To have one run across your face is not unusual.

4. A tent. Fairly good in bad weather, but you get wet, and so does most of your stuff in downpours. But you have your privacy. No bugs. No mice. But! It weighs four pounds dry, and more wet. It is a massive pain to put one up in a downpour. Four pounds makes this the heaviest one item you carry. Many, and I really think most, thru-hikers send their tents home. They go with the tarp and look for lean-tos in bad weather. It is a matter of weight. I sent mine home weeks ago.

5. A hostel or a bunkhouse. Along the Trail, people, churches, and community groups rent, or in some cases, offer for free, bunks and hostels. They provide small beds with, sometimes, a rubber mattress. That's it. For linen, you use your sleeping bag. Electricity and plumbing might exist, but only centrally. A half-step up from a shelter. Bunkhouses cost between $5 and $15 per night.

6. Hiker-friendly motels. $25 to $35 per night. Dumps usually. I can afford to get a room alone. But most of my friends, males and females, would share motel rooms. Everyone sleeps together in camp. These motels are only lean-tos with walls.

7. Motels. The Micro-tel and many budget hotels are popular. We run into these when the AT crosses an interstate highway.

8. Bed and Breakfast. Usually not suitable for hikers. Or should I say the other way around. We are filthy, we stink, and we knock things over a lot, pretty lamps, for example. But some B&Bs welcome us. Hikers who can afford it do seek out a B&B from time to time.

9. A friend's home is the absolute best.

I have done all of the above. I grab a bed whenever I can. Sleeping on the ground or the hard surface of a shelter is tough. It is hard to sleep well, and you remain exhausted. I can't abuse myself if I am doing this for the long haul, and I am.

E-mail #31–Map Marker #19

I don't know how to describe today's hike. But to start with, I am furious.

The local hiking club crossed the line with Dragon's Tooth. The AT should be a challenge, a test, difficult, but it should not be overtly and purposely dangerous. There is no other description for Dragon's Tooth.

There were several steps where a mistake would have led to a traumatic injury. A few would be fatal, and I am not exaggerating.

This was exacerbated by the fact that the Trail managers sent you over a multitude of pointless ups and downs—PUDs—before you got to the Tooth. So it was guaranteed you would be exhausted when you got there.

I often look just 15 yards away from these PUDs, and there would be a place where a reasonable trail is cut by the local hikers, but the trail club sends the AT through the boulder-infested PUDs just for the fun of it.

I talked to two southbound hikers who felt the Tooth was much too difficult and dangerous, so they stopped and turned around and walked back a few miles to a road and will yellow-blaze around this mountain. They were told of the dangers by a past thru-hiker, and when they saw it for themselves, they turned around.

While I am pretty well wired to hiker's news, I know nothing about Dragon's Tooth. There is nothing in the *Hiker Guide,* nothing posted on the Trail. Coming northbound, I am sucked into this danger. Exhausted by the 10 to 20 ridiculous PUDs, which grow harder, suddenly I am hanging over a precipice with few handholds and certain serious injury if I slip.

To help things, it is drizzling, then raining, then pouring.

If I choose to go back, it's 12 miles, six hours, and all those PUDs to do again. I hope this precipice is the only dangerous one I find. But it's not. They get worse. My toes are on rock; my heels are hanging in the air.

What kind of organization would put a person into this level of danger? No warning, no alternate trail offered. Certain rock faces have no—repeat no—hand holds. So iron rungs jut out from the stones. I hang my trekking poles around my wrists and move very slowly. I feel certain that going back now will be more dangerous than moving on.

I move at a snail's pace, but I move. After what seems to be an hour of traversing the cliffs, scaling large boulders, and hanging on the side of this mountain, I spot a real path ahead. I tell myself not to get careless now. I continue moving slowly and I reach the path. This path, white-blazed, leads back where I came from! Can you believe it? This Trail purposely wound through the danger for the experience. It doesn't go anywhere!

I was so angry. If a trail club member had shown his face, I would have relieved him of some teeth. I'm not kidding.

Wanda Mitchell, the hostel owner, later told me of a recent very serious accident here. I was not surprised.

This should never be a life-jeopardizing activity. I agree with the two coming from the south, the club crossed the line.

Many of us are members of the ATC; we are told our dues are directed toward safety. Bullshit.

I have seen enough bad judgment; I simply feel they cannot be trusted. This has a lonely, scariness to it. Because if you are alone in the wilderness, these clubs are your companions. Not to trust them, their blazes, their signs, leaves us with a sense of being abandoned.

When I finished the day, I passed 700 miles. One-third through. When I cool off, I'll be happy about that.

E-mail #32–Map Marker #20

Today, May 4, I walk into Catawba, Virginia, and I am treated to the fabulous hospitality of Wanda and Joe Mitchell at the Four Pines Hikers Hostel. The hostel is a converted three-bay garage. They added a hot and cold shower, and a pot bellied stove. These are over-the-top luxuries. But it's Wanda and Joe who make this place special. I ask if they have a private room. (I longed for a night without snoring or varmints). They didn't, but they did offer me their basement. Queen bed, TV, Jacuzzi, and bathroom. I was also invited to eat with them, with Wanda's magnificent breakfast and dinner. This is much more than anything I could have hoped for. They are more than Trail angels; they make for their guests a feeling of home for a while—something we desperately need.

Joe is making a run with a pile of hikers in the bed of his pickup to the all-you-can–eat restaurant, while Wanda and I sit on the front porch and look up at Dragons Tooth. We can actually see a speck on the Tooth. A hiker. In an hour or two, he will be down, off the mountain, and probably pissed-off. He will see a little wooden sign with an arrow pointing right, "Four Pines Hostel," it says. Take the right, buddy.

E-mail #33

"See you down the Trail." This is what thru-hikers say to each other, we don't say goodbye. I like it, particularly, because it's often true. We continue to run into our colleagues over and over again, when we never expect to.

I like "see you down the Trail." It's our version of *au revoir*—which means 'til we meet again. It's positive. It suggests a future.

The worst good-bye is "have a good one." Huh? What the shit does that mean? I hate it. It's generic and disrespectful.

Is it pet peeve time?

E-mail #34

Here is an update on some of my characters.

The *Flying Pork Chop* lives! And it appears he is doing fine. His entries in the registers put him about 6 or 7 days ahead of me, moving well. He stayed at some of the hostels and places I stayed, and I am able to keep up with him through the hostel managers and owners. He is like Johnny Appleseed. No one forgets him. He spreads good will and good feelings wherever he goes. He seems to be everyone's favorite.

Pinecone has slowed down. He is only a couple of days ahead of me. The little shit is burning out. Good.

Pinetree is either gone or far behind—no news.

Sly and Stone are not able to keep up those twenties. Dog's pads, the bottom of their feet, need rest from rocks, and Virginia has a bunch. Stone, on the other hand, needs action. He almost got locked up in Blacksburg for mooning a bar. But he is so damn charming. According to the story, it ended with him and the cop exchanging e-mails and promising to stay in touch.

Turkey Bacon is still unlikable, but moving on. He is a tough little guy. I respect him.

April is the most interesting person. Now that the calendar has turned to May, she is calling herself *April-May*. No one knows if April is her Trail name or her real name. There is no one thing pretty about her, but the package is very fetching. Stone is smitten. But she is a better and faster hiker than Stone, and when he bores her, she takes off, literally. She raises her hand, says "See you down the Trail" and she is gone. She writes poetry in the shelter registers; she listens to everything and remembers everything. And there is something deeply sad about her. She also seems desperately poor. When approaching a town, she will sleep in a shelter just outside of town and then hike through. If she stays in town, it will only be if it has a free hostel. April is spiritual and mysterious.

Jeff, my section-hiker friend, finished his section and went home. He was a thru-hiker in his heart. And he wanted to go on with us. He is an interesting person and a terrific listener. He can get more information out of people during a conversation than anyone I have ever seen. Talking to him is better than going to a psychiatrist.

He built a business with his own hands and sold it. If all goes well with the closing, he will be rich. Good luck to a really good guy.

The Mass Four are four kids who went to the University of Massachusetts. They are the only group that I have met that I think will reach Katahdin together. They have the right group dynamic. Devin is in charge. He is smart, smooth, and charismatic. He is not overbearing, but he is in charge. Andy is the master sergeant. Tough and strong, but also with a heart of gold. Molly is the brains of the group. Quiet, but when she speaks, all listen. Jeff is the wonder boy—their personality. He is responsible for morale.

Because they have a group trail name, they don't have individual trail names. This speaks volumes, and it also is one of the reasons I think they will make it—together. They have placed their identity in the group, not individually.

E-mail #35

Dana visits in Catawba, and says I am more peaceful. Bullshit. I am the same old asshole, just going at two miles an hour.

Dana and I drive over to Blacksburg to get Mexican food. There in the middle of the road is a black bear. He looks at the car and lumbers off. No time for a picture, but I snap a couple anyway. Can you believe it? Thousands of hikers covering the wilderness who want to see a bear, and Dana spots one, from a car, while going to get Mexican. She is blessed; I've always thought so.

E-mail #36–Map Marker #21

The Trail is running back and forth across the Blue Ridge Parkway. The Parkway is a priceless gift the National Park Service has given us.

Yesterday, I was completely lost in deep fog. The blazes were impossible to see. I kept my head down and tried to stay on the foot path. If I came to another trail crossing, I guessed which one was the AT. I came upon the Parkway. I knew it would continue to intersect with the AT, so I headed north on the Parkway. I picked up a couple of other stranded hikers who were also stalled.

It worked out. What a relief. The fog lifted and we were in a mountain paradise. We soon found the AT. When we entered the canopy of the AT, I missed the openness of the Parkway.

The Trail seems claustrophobic now. This time of year on the Parkway there is almost no traffic; everyone is over on I-81 going some place. The Blue Ridge Parkway has a 35-mile per hour speed limit and allows no trucks. This is not a highway for someone going somewhere, unless that somewhere happens to be tranquility.

I hear the Parkway is packed during leaf season and camping season, when the kids are first out of school. But on May 8, there are just some lost thru-hikers.

I hate it that the AT experiences so little of the Parkway. Again, I am at odds with the ATC.

Along the Parkway, I met Scott, the brother-in-law of my sister-in-law. My sister-in-law, Lisa, said he wanted to visit me along the Trail. I had met him once before and liked him, and any visit was welcome. We met near the Foot Bridge over the James River. Scott brought bourbon, ice, Cokes and real glass glasses. But most important, he brought a *car*. What a great afternoon. Scott is my hero.

E-mail #37–Map Marker #22

The walking stick

Things happen on the Trail that I am convinced can happen nowhere else. Too wonderful, almost unbelievable.

I end my hike today—17 miles, a hard 17 miles, and at the very end of the Trail, I find a walking stick propped against a tree. My eye is drawn to it by a nearby squirrel. I have learned that a quick ten-minute catnap revives my energy. So I take the walking stick and my two trekking poles to make a pyramid with the tree and lean against them for a nap in a meadow area.

When I awake, for the first time, I take a closer look at the walking stick. Someone cares about this stick; it is well crafted. Sanded and lacquered several layers. Up and down the shaft is writing. It appears to be burned in by a wood-burning set.

It reads something like this: "I am from Springer Mountain, Georgia. I am going to Katahdin, Maine. Please pick me up, and carry me awhile. Don't take me off the AT. If you like, drop a note to my friend at the following address. Tell him where we met, and where you left me. When I reach Katahdin, my friend will bring me home; you can let him know I'm there with the following e-mail address." At the bottom of the walking stick I see the address and the e-mail address.

Because I am leaving the Trail for the day, I can't take the walking stick very far. I lean it on a tree, I look back, and I leave it to its journey. There is a spirit of honor on the trail. There is no one overseeing thru-hikers. They walk the Trail, receive their 2,000-mile patch, and adopt forever the title thru-hiker, totally on the honor system. This spirit extends to much of what makes the hike special, and allows stories like the walking stick to abound. This walking stick, by itself, has come from Springer Mountain, 810 miles.

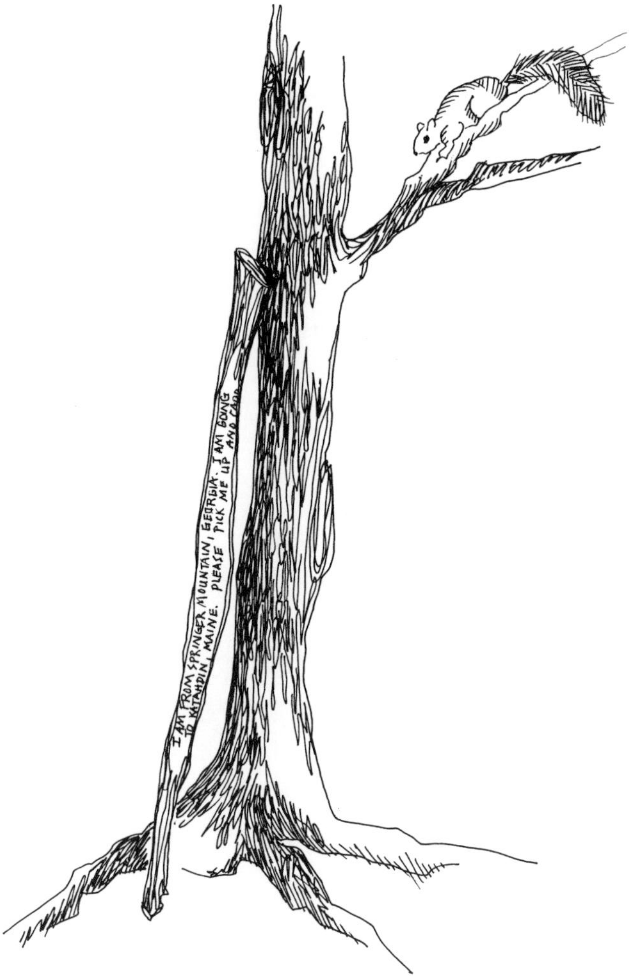

– A squirrel caught my attention, and then I saw the walking stick –

E-mail #38–Map Marker #23

The Renegade Angel

Renegade and I have two of the coldest beers on the planet. Old Milwaukee in a secret cooler, iced for three days by the time I showed up.

Renegade is having his eleventh annual cookout that he holds for hikers. Hotdogs, hamburgers, eggs and bacon if it's in the morning, and really, really cold soft drinks. He is easily the master of trail angels. He set up shop at one of the road crossings with three portable stoves, six coolers, eight comfy camping chairs, tables and tons of groceries.

When I arrive, he is in a quiet period, and I am his only customer. It is around 2:30 in the afternoon, very hot. He is willing to cook me something, but I am more interested in a cold beer. I don't know about the secret cooler, but it seems to make sense. "Renegade, if a man was to put a ten in your supplies-tip jar mightn't a beer appear?" It does. We sit and talk about a number of his interesting customers over the years. About the three huge football players who were hiking in dresses. About a girl who was out of money who set up camp nearby so she could eat there every day. He fed her for three days, then she disappeared. It is a pleasant way to spend an afternoon, a little break from hiking. After taking his and my picture, I head down the Trail.

E-mail #39–Map Marker #24

The dragon strikes.

I ran into good friends of Dana and her brother David. The Oz family. He's *Tin Man*, and his wife, *Ruby Slippers*, and their dog, *Toto*. They were folks I didn't know, but I know them now. It is a gift to talk about home and family with these strangers, who would never be strangers again.

I pass a highway then, shortly after, come upon a hiker going in the opposite direction. I know that he was a north-bounder and he is heading south. He is limping. He tells me he slipped on a rock and twisted his knee. He is going back to the highway I just crossed to hitch to a doctor. I look at his knee. He would be going home. His thru-hike is over. In one of my lives, I was a high school football coach I have seen enough knees to know. His thru-hike is over. The dragon struck.

A little later, I realize I should have carried his pack to the highway. I'm ashamed that I didn't. It is not the hikers way to let him limp on alone.

This isn't my best moment.

E-mail #40

A finch is just like us.

Along the way, just off the Parkway, I stay at the Dutch House, a hikers bed and breakfast. There is nothing Dutch about it. Lois and Earl Arnold are Texans; their house is made of logs. Oh well, they call it the Dutch House. And that's okay with me.

The place is great, as are the Arnolds. A goldfinch just flew into their glass door. Lois says it happens often. He knocked himself out. Lois picks him up and holds him in her hands. Being upright and warmth helps them recover, she says. The finch is male; therefore, it is colorful, gold and black, painted by the hand of Mother Nature. His beak is slightly open. He is totally still, but his heart is racing.

She holds the bird right-side up and strokes him with one finger. Finally, it chirps a bit, and then she lays it on the feeder. In a minute, he flies away. Lois smiles and goes about making our dinner.

We try to see where the finch would go next, but he is soon indistinguishable as he joins his friends. When was the first time Lois picked up one of these little guys? And what made her do it? I'll have to ask. It's good there are people like Lois. They seem to congregate around the Trail.

Lois cooks a tasty meal for ten dollars. We sit down and get to know each other. On the opposite end of the table from me is a hiker I had not met before. He is quiet, a listener; he is poised, and when he speaks obviously smart. He has an aura of gentleness and you immediately like and trust him. Very important in a hiker.

Pipe Wrench is to become a great friend.

E-mail #41

I fear the dragon.

In his cave, I think now I can see him. I can hear his ragged breathing like a monstrous locomotive, moving ever so slowly.

At any time, the dragon can reach out with his monstrous claws and sweep some of us off the Trail.

My dragon might be a neuroma, between the second and third toes of my right foot. A neuroma is a pissed-off nerve trapped between two bones. So pissed-off, it swells to about the size of a pencil eraser. Any time these toe knucklebones move closer to each other, they pinch the neuroma. Mucho pain.

I have had this before, on my left foot. Finally, the pain was so great, I had the neuroma removed surgically.

Can't walk for two weeks, can't run for two months. This would definitely be a dragon, and end my thru-hike.

Now Mr. Right Foot wants his own neuroma. Months ago, my good doctor pushed back the inevitable with a cortisone shot. It worked for about 90 days. But the pain has returned. He shot it again, reluctantly, just before I left on the AT. It worked again—sort of. The pain lingered, but was less. Not gone like before.

Each day the dragon grows. The pain becomes worse. For now, I am okay. Should I get another shot? First of all, I am not sure my doctor would do it this close to the last one. Also, the last one didn't work so well.

I fear the dragon.

E-mail #42–Map Marker #24

I take a break.

The Blue Ridge Parkway becomes Skyline Drive at Rockfish Gap. I take a break here, some zeros.

Thursday, I go home for a planned trip. I can't wait. I worry about being sucked off the Trail by my home. But I don't think so. There are too many things yet to see.

For the second time, the hikers who surround me will move on. I am truly sad about this, but anxious too. I will return to meet new friends.

"See you down the Trail," I think. I pull out the little stone I picked up at Springer Mountain. It is cool to the touch.

E-mail #43–Map Markers #25–26

Memorial Day. Back on the Trail.

Moving through Shenandoah. I stop at a shelter and look at the register. I don't know anyone who had signed recently. This has a really lonely feeling to it.

I looked further back—then further—finally a name or two I knew. A week ahead of me. Gone forever probably.

My only hope of being reunited with an old friend would be Trail Days in Damascus. I did not go, of course, but lots of folks I know took multiple zeros to hitch back to Damascus and go to Trail Days. Trail Days is a big hikers convention/party. The word is that it was a blast.

If they stayed long enough, I might catch some of them at Harpers Ferry.

The Shenandoahs are a nice change of pace. The Trail here is not easy, which is a surprise because we were told that it was. It is not terribly difficult either. But you earn your miles.

What's different are the waysides, the cabins, the lodges, and the campgrounds. A wayside is a general store/restaurant. There is one every 10 miles or so on Skyline Drive. You need little water, and no food in your pack, making it very light.

Plan a little, and you will have a roof over your head almost every night. A cabin room, a tent cabin, a lodge room or a prepared campsite with facilities. You can eat virtually all your meals at a restaurant or waysides. I like it as a break. Too much of it would kill the AT adventure. But 105 miles is just right.

I start thinking about finishing Virginia, then West Virginia and Maryland.

After Harpers Ferry, West Virginia, there is Maryland. A total of 40 miles. Some of the wild-asses do it in one hike. A 24-hour blitz. It is called Maryland Madness or some call it the Maryland Challenge. 40 miles would kill me. And besides I want to go into Pennsylvania in good shape. Pennsylvania is tough, and not to be fooled with.

Because I came close to stepping on a big snake, orange in color (a copperhead?), I spot things on the Trail that are serpentine in form. One thing I notice is tubular and snakelike, but fuzzy. It catches my eye, but it soon is obvious it isn't alive. It is some kind of growth or deposit.

I come across this young girl poking one of these things with a stick. "What is that?" I asked.

"Owl puke," she said. "When owls eat rats and mice, they digest everything but the hair, it collects over time, then they puke it up."

Too much information, my face said. She doesn't notice. She is too busy poking the puke.

E-mail #44–Map Markers #27

Good-bye Virginia

There are too many snakes. It's spring and I guess they slither about more in the spring. I've seen four so far, and that is too many, because I am certain there were many more I didn't see. And they are all venomous killers. As far as I am concerned every snake I see is poisonous. The deadly rattle-cobra-moccasin. Another one today. Big. Lying across the Trail.

I have learned about the message center of my brain. As far as emergencies are concerned, I am a courtesy copy. Only an afterthought.

My eyes pick up the snake and send a signal to my brain. Mr. Brain goes straight to the muscles. "Shut down," he says. "Okay guys, good job. Now I have to tell the dufus that he almost stepped on a snake." Finally, he informs me why I am standing still. By the time I recognize this is a snake, I am still, not walking anymore. My brain stopped my movement before it informed me why.

I am leaving the state of Virginia, and I am ready. Over 500 miles, a full fourth of the AT is enough. But I have to tell ya, Virginia, you do it right. Your land is beautiful. You respect the Trail and those who tread on it. Your people are generous and considerate. You have preserved a flavor of your history. You are a classy, sort of an Ivy League southern state.

But VA releases us grudgingly. We walk on the border between Virginia and West Virginia for miles. Literally every other step alternating the two states. Finally, the AT turns hard west and Virginia is behind us. Thank you, Virginia, I will return.

E-mail #45–Map Marker #28

Harpers Ferry drips with history.
For a guy like me, I love it.

The most defining battle of the Civil War is just over the hill.

Harpers Ferry itself is monumentally strategic. It sits high on the confluence of the Shenandoah and Potomac Rivers. It has historically been a center for munitions manufacturing. For these reasons, Harpers Ferry flew both the Union and the Confederate flags more than once during the Civil War.

Also, prior to the Civil War, there was John Brown. He captured one of the munitions buildings, thinking black freeman and slaves would rally to his rescue. A U.S. officer named Robert E. Lee put down the rebellion. While the effort failed, John Brown became the icon for the struggle ahead. It is not unusual for historical icons to have been flawed people, and John Brown certainly had been one of those.

Also, Harpers Ferry gave birth to the first predominantly black college, Storer College. History seems to seep out of the pores of this little, fragile town perched on the most eastern rocks of West Virginia.

Dana visits, and we drive to Antietam. Being a Southerner, I say Sharpsburg—northern generals named their battles for the nearest river—classical West Point training. Southern generals named their battles for the nearest town, in this case Sharpsburg. But the names of the dead—they shared. There were families, even brothers, who were at war and on opposite sides.

The battle of Antietam was beyond horrible. Massive in scope. A bottomless vessel of spilled blood. In one hour, more Americans were killed at Antietam, than all three previous U.S. wars combined.

At Bloody Road, the Union and Confederate armies found themselves pointing their muskets at each other, not 20 feet apart, with only split rail fencing for protection. Hundreds died in minutes.

Thousands of wounded were visible in the open farmland. The officers would call a cease fire and all would lay down their weapons and walk out onto the battlefield and tend to the dead, dying and wounded. Confederate and Union soldiers would be shoulder-to-shoulder often helping each other with a wounded man. They would shake the hand of their enemy. Exchange a word or two, some tobacco, and then return to their ranks for another round of horror.

There were too many dead to tend to. Untold hundreds were left in the fields of Antietam, their remains untouched for years.

The Confederate Army, after moving north across the Shenendoah River, fought their foe, but only to a standoff and retreated in the dead of night. Unbelievable carnage occurred during the retreat.

The battlefield is preserved. The little church, which was the epicenter of the battle, still stands. You can go on a driving tour, which goes on for miles. Dana and I leave; we drive through the little, sad town of Sharpsburg and say good-bye to Antietam.

E-mail #46–Map Marker #

Harper's Ferry and the Canal

West Virginia is finished, on to Maryland. Picture a mountain that dips dramatically into a beautiful river. But just before it gets to the river, man gets involved. He builds a railroad, then a canal. If you have a canal, you have to have a towpath where horses, mules, and sometimes men pull on long ropes attached to the barges laden with cargo. The towpath is an isthmus between the canal and the Potomac River.

A century and a half ago, the railroad and the canal competed for the same cargo and transportation business. Both coming from the East Coast going west. This Harpers Ferry place was the spot they came.

The canal came closest to the settlement of Harper's Ferry at Lock 33. The water was raised in the Lock, and the barge was towed farther into, what was then, the wild and growing west. Impressive engineering for the 19th Century. The train was always breaking down, the canal was much more reliable. But when the train worked, it was fast. And we Americans have always loved speed.

When the Civil War came, speed was of the essence. The canal system was shut down—forever. The train system still thrives—both passenger and freight.

The canals are still there. Some have water. The towpaths are bike paths, and it is still called the C&O Canal. The Chesapeake and Ohio. I walk by it for hours, and stop and study Lock 33. I picture the barge being pulled into it and raised, then pulled farther west.

The water in the canal is only 15 yards or so away from the water in the Potomac, but often higher. A few of the locks are operable and tourists can take a ride.

I finish the day, doing 18 miles. New shoes today; they worked fine.

I miss Dana terribly the day after she leaves. I am starting to miss Sassafras, and I wonder how she is doing. Tallulah's memory is fading a bit. I wish it wouldn't, but it is. The circle of life, Elton John says.

E-mail #47

Old friends

In Harpers Ferry, I hear about old friends and see some others. I hear that Stone is giving up on the thru-hike. He can't finish before school starts. He will finish the AT as a section-hiker, skipping over Vermont and New Hampshire as he has done those before. He will go on to Katahdin and finish, and then return to school in Arizona.

Stone's home life is rough. When he gets nurtured on the Trail, he sticks. He spent seven days at a friendly hostel eliminating any chance of completing his thru-hike. But by doing so, he fills some other holes in his life.

Harpers Ferry is hilly and steep. Upstairs on a porch swing at the outfitter, while I am trying on some new boots, I hear "Bearfoot." And there is Stone, down on the street. We agree to get together for a beer, and he heads up the hill, leaning against it with each step.

Sly, as always, is about 20 feet ahead of him. I think she turns to look up at me. This is the last time I see Sly.

Sparrow and *Gunslinger* left the Trail; maybe to come back later, *Rawhide* is in mourning. He secretly loves Sparrow and everyone knows it except the three of them. April moves on. Giggles and *Highwater* are moving well toward their native Canada. They seemed genuinely happy to see me; it has been since the Smokies when I last saw them.

The headquarters of the ATC is in Harpers Ferry. I drop by, ask a few questions, and they take my picture. I am assigned a number.

As a northbound thru-hiker, I was 168.

Only 167 people are ahead of me this year. Probably a little less than half of that is behind me. It seems like a small number, considering how many started. Thousands down to a few hundred, and more than half-way to go.

I look at all the pictures taken by the ATC staff, and I see the Flying Porkchop. I would have never recognized him. He looks great. But I can't help but think of all those whose pictures are not there in the book. Except on weekends, there will be no more full shelters or hostels. Now, hikers I meet will be tougher, focused. I will miss the dreamers.

E-mail #48–Map Marker #30

I duck under a tornado.

I cross the Mason-Dixon Line into Pennsylvania. So far it is pretty tame. Plenty of rocks, but nothing I haven't seen before. The rocks are supposed to be terrible north of a town named Clinton. (I refuse to get caught up in the obvious puns. Tempted, but I refuse.)

At the B&B back in Harpers Ferry where Dana and I stayed, we met a couple who seemed to be too good to be true, Brian and Kim. They were funny, interesting, interested—just really neat. They asked me to call when I went through Penn-Mar which is near their house. They promised to bring me a slice of homemade pie.

Unfortunately, I pass through Penn-Mar early in the morning.

That afternoon there are tornado warnings and the ranger recommends that we get off the Trail, and try to find enclosed shelter. A bunch of us go to U.S. 30 and hitch to a motel. After I settle in, I put a call into Brian and tell him why I hadn't called earlier.

The tornados, in fact, did come. And they moved through the area. Finally, they were east of us, and life reemerged.

About 9:00, I get a call in the motel room indicating I have a visitor at the front desk. There were Brian and Kim and their daughter, Alicia. And also a chocolate pie with graham cracker crust.

My favorite.

What can I say?

E-mail #49–Map Marker #31

A 20, one of many

There are no easy 20-mile days. But the 20 today was uplifting. Bookended by two state parks, Caledonia and Pine Grove Furnace, these 20 miles are beautiful. The Trail runs through blooming mountain laurel and rhododendron. The rains yesterday left the forest an assault of green. The smells are equal to the colors.

At the end of the 20, there is a public swimming pool. Kids making noises they make only when they are in a pool. And a snack bar! Hot dogs and ice cream!

No 20 is easy, but I'll always remember this day fondly.

E-mail #50–Map Marker #31

The mid-way marker

In the early- to mid-1800s, the transportation system could not move the thousands of tons of iron ore unearthed from the mines. So when it was discovered, the smelting operation was moved to the ore. Hundreds of small smelting furnaces sprang up in the wilderness of Virginia, Maryland and Pennsylvania. To fuel the furnaces charcoal was needed, which the forests provided. Hiking through these parts today, you'll find huge charcoal pits and rock furnaces in ruins. The furnace in Pine Grove Park is preserved as it was 150 years ago.

But the monument I am interested in is not the furnace. There it is, in a darkened part of the Trail. My first impression is that it looks like a totem pole. About 12 feet tall, the ATC crest at the top, a register box in the middle, and two arrows. One pointing north, one pointing south. This is the mid-way marker.

Graybeard and *Grey Hound* walk up. They are motel friends and section-hikers who I met when we were hiding from the tornado. Grey Hound, the wife, thru-hiked three years ago. She and her husband are doing some of her favorite sections. This is one of them. We take pictures of each other, and then we sign the register. The mid-way marker is hypothetical, and we all know it. The Trail is constantly being re-routed, which would require constantly moving the marker up and down the Trail.

But this is nice. I appreciate it. It really does give me a sense of accomplishment, though it is still daunting as to what is ahead. I thank the ATC for this gesture.

Graybeard and Grey Hound stick around. I move on. I don't know why, but I feel a crushing loneliness. I put my head down, lean on my poles, and push north.

— At the
Mid-Way Marker,
I felt a
crushing loneliness —

SECTION TWO

E-mail #1–Map Marker #32

Boiling Springs

I had never heard of it. A tiny village with a lake in the middle. The lake is surrounded by century-old mansions that have been converted to bed & breakfasts, restaurants and stores.

One of the restaurants is first class, but not so fancy that it is put-offish. There is also an outfitter, whose owner happens to be a fly-fishing expert. I discover, while buying a few provisions, that Boiling Springs is a trout fishing mecca. And it survives by catering to fly fishermen who come out of D.C. and Philly. There is a hand-dipped ice cream store, even swans. Boiling Springs is a magical spot in the middle of the Southern Pennsylvania farmland. The AT goes through the middle of town.

I slack-pack when I discover Boiling Springs.

Remember slack-packing? Basically, it is hiking a few sections without your backpack. It is only possible if you are in a highly civilized area with roads crossing the Trail. The B&B owner picks you up a day out of town, then you stay at the B&B that night, he then takes you back to that spot where he picked you up. Now you hike into town, and your pack is waiting for you in your room. The next day, he shuttles you 15 or 18 miles forward and you hike back to the B&B. The third day he takes you to the same spot he took you to the second day, with your pack. You say goodbye and head north. Two days of slack-packing. Three nights in the B&B. Three evenings of walking around Boiling Springs.

A hikers holiday.

E-mail #2

Hiking techniques

When I started the Trail, my attitude was *hiking*? You mean *walking*? You know, right foot, left foot, and so on. Wrong. Hiking, like any other physical pursuit, has correct and incorrect techniques.

Your pack changes your center of gravity—a lot. You often don't put your feet where you intend. You miss open spots by inches and step on the side of a rock, turning your ankle unexpectedly. Your normal walk will not do.

Upright walking does not give you any shock absorber effect, and/or room for error. Straight up means straight down when something slips. So you lean forward, compensating for your pack, and crouch with bent knees. I call it my Groucho Marx walk. This allows your head to stay reasonably level while your hips and legs absorb the ups and downs.

You seldom lock your knees, as you normally do with each step. Locking your knees gives leg muscles rest. In a hard hike, my legs seldom come to this rest the entire day.

Your mind has taken over civilized walking. It knows, about five steps in advance, that a foot is going to step on or over something, and it knows when, and with which foot.

On most days, I have to override that automatic system, and tell feet where to go each step as it happens. I have been astonished by how much concentration hiking requires. Particularly difficult trails require a high degree of concentration, sometimes for many unbroken hours.

My friends say it must be great to have all this time to think. Well, it is, but not while I'm hiking the hard trails. It is usually at night that I have time to think. Letting your mind wander on a hard trail can result in a hike-ending injury. And mistakes always hurt. Truthfully, I have 10 things that hurt from the knees down. Almost always because I let my mind wander.

Going downhill, in normal walking, requires leaning against the hill. Leaning back, in other words. You will quickly be on your ass leaning back on the Trail on downhills. Shockingly, you lean forward. It takes much practice to lean forward going downhill. And it is more than a little scary. Lead with your poles, come down on your toes, not your heels.

Trekking poles are a must. Using the poles, your weight is distributed to four points. If one slips, you still have three points to keep you upright. With no poles, one slips, one remains. You might correct your balance, but not always; eventually the odds will run out. One pole is better than none, two are better than one. For a stroll in the woods, pick up a walking stick off the ground. For a hike, buy trekking poles.

Rock hiking means you don't touch soil, sometimes for hundreds of steps. Rock to rock, to rock. You step on big rocks the size of a throw rug in your bathroom, big enough to accept your whole foot, down to small points of a rock where only one square inch of your shoe is in contact. Also there is the blade edge of a rock; toward you, perpendicular, at an angle, and always slanted. On blades you try to place the arch of your foot directly on the blade. Often with mixed results. The worst is when you know your step will be between two or more rocks. Now your ankle bone will get a wake-up call. Your ankles are constantly slanting, rotating, sometimes twisting over. Your knees are compensating, sometimes too much.

By the end of the day, you are exhausted. Your feet hurt everywhere. Your knees ache. And the concentration required completes the exhaustion.

Hiking straight up hill takes long powerful strides. I am good up hill. I am not an overly fast straight-ahead hiker. I am slow down hill. Down hill is hardest on the knees. My knees are my weakest link leg-wise. I am now wearing a knee brace. Most people make up time on the downhills. Not me.

Mathematically the AT works well at a 12-mile a day average. Six months, then add your zeros. I am trying to average 15 miles a day. The math then becomes five months plus zeros. The last two weeks, I have averaged 17, but I know I will go slowly in Northern Pennsylvania, the Whites, and in Maine.

My weakest hiking technique is sliding my feet too low. In other words, a good hiker makes bicycle lifts as he steps. I don't, and I pay for it over and over again. Stumble stumps, stumble stones, and roots get me. You can't spot and avoid them all. I stumble a lot. For the rest of my life, I will recall Stone losing patience with my stumbles. "Pick up your feet, Bearfoot."

The most fluid hiker in our group is Pipe Wrench.

I have always respected the tenacity necessary to complete the AT. I now respect the athleticism required. I now can spot and admire a good hiker when I see one. I am a long, long way from being one.

E-mail #3–Map Marker #33

Why me?

How did the stars align where the Machine-Gun Giggler's hike and mine reconnected? We are camped together tonight, he is driving me nuts. Hee, hee, hee.

E-mail #4–Map Marker #34

Pennsylvania is hell.

Pennsylvania's reputation is well earned. South is pretty and smooth sailing. North is hell—rock hell. Every kind of rock. Little and sharp. Big and slippery. Very deep except for a sharp point. Rip-rap. Boulders—slime covered.

Today's hike is between Port Clinton and Lehigh Gap. Some of the fun is called Knife's Blade. Other sections: Quarry Gap, Hawk Rock, Table Rock, Stoney Mountain. You get the point.

Hiking in Pennsylvania hurts. It's slow. You fall. But then suddenly you are high up, looking at villages and farmland. And you stop and admire. Until you look down again at the Trail, which you must.

Knife's Blade is just that. A blade. Two high sharp edges on the top of the mountain, leaning together. The edge is probably six inches wide. Just enough room for your boot. It is on top of Blue Mountain and it is slippery because of green lichen that covers some of the rock, particularly in the shade. It is the only time I have had vertigo on the Trail.

But my most hated section is known as Bake Oven Knob. It is a boulder field of acres, maybe hundreds of acres, where I simply never touch soil. Each step is at risk. Because there are few trees, blazes are painted on the rocks. They sometimes wash off. I get lost three times. This is one of those times I wish I had a hiking partner.

The third time I get lost, I would have cried if I wasn't laughing. What an incredible, frustrating and overwhelming feeling. It is also sincerely scary. You know you have lost the Trail. You look left and right. Maybe you can spot it off in the distance. Maybe you can spot a blaze. If you can, then you can bushwhack over to the Trail. But all too often you see what might be the Trail, isn't. Your other alternative is to turn around and go back. But that is not a sure route either. Lost means lost. Sometimes I have been lost for hours. My anxiety rises. This is how people die. It hurts like hell to take a step, but I must take a hunch or go back and look for the Trail again. I go back and find it and move on. The day ends.

Two more rock sections in Pennsylvania. Two more rock sections in New Jersey, then things return to what we call normal.

E-mail #5–Map Marker #35

Screw you and the horse you rode in on.

I am sure I am not the first person to feel this way, or even write about it.

People become like their land. Pennsylvanians, for example, are tough people. Some would say hard. They had a ferocious reputation as fighters in the Civil War.

They are not like other people along the Trail. Not hospitable, not very curious. If some nut wants to walk over 2,000 miles over rocks and snakes, just let him. It's not any of their business, and they don't really give a shit.

There are parts of this state that are downright depressing. Duncannon and Port Clinton among them. I hike into Port Clinton and say hello to three straight people who do not respond in any way. Two dogs crash into chain link fences trying to get at me, obviously trained to maim.

The lady at the Port Clinton Hotel tells me to give her my driver's license, and take the room she assigns me sight unseen or get the hell out of her place.

The town has no cell service, no public phones, no ATM, and signs everywhere that the use of their phones ain't gonna happen. Even if you're a customer. Cut off from the world, and screw you and the horse you rode in on.

The Trail is just as inhospitable. The mountain at Lehigh Gap is absolutely unique, and I am glad of that.

This mountain is a pile of rocks, as if God dropped millions of them, all sizes, until they piled up into a mountain. No soil at all. To get up it, or down it, you step rock to rock, on rocks, resting on rocks.

Sometimes these rocks hold your weight. Often they don't. They slip, flip, or turn. Your foot goes with the rock. Ankles simply go with the foot. Real sprains and tumbles, you fall down on one knee, or both knees, and you fall a lot.

There are parts of this mountain that require all-fours climbing. Dangerous in terms of hands, elbows, ankles, knees, and feet. You're going to get cuts and scrapes. Some could be serious, not as dangerous as Albert Mountain or Dragon's Tooth, but it is almost guaranteed that you will leave this mountain hurt.

In my case, my left knee was doing great, but not now. It is now in its worst shape of the trip. Of course, it pisses me off, but not at the ATC or at the Trail Club that maintains this section. There is actually no alternative. I had to come down Lehigh Gap from the south, then cross the bridge, and go up the other side of the Lehigh River. This is where the mountain is. If you are going to climb it, you're going to have to go up it as it is. Like it or not, to go up, you climb these rocks.

I'm just pissed off at the situation. It hurts, and getting hurt pisses me off.

When I told a Pennsylvanian, he smiled. Typical. They love to see out-of-staters getting hurt.

Once reaching the top of this mountain, I enter the Palmerton EPA Superfund Site. I hike for two hours through devastation like nothing you have ever seen. It appears to be post Hiroshima. Unbelievable. Sixteen square miles of poison. I wish I could hold my breath. The top of this mountain was killed by a century of zinc manufacturing in the valley. The smoke rose with the prevailing winds being north. The mountain was in the way. It was killed. The top of the rocks look normal, the bottoms are black. Scary. All vegetation dead.

Pennsylvania. I leave it tomorrow. I don't know a hiker who will be sorry to leave Pennsylvania. Once we pass the mid-point marker, there is nothing redeeming. The towns are ugly; the people are inhospitable. The Trail is, well, Pennsylvania.

We have decided that Pennsylvania is like an emergency appendectomy. It hurts, it has to be done. When it's over you are no better off, you have a scar, and you got rid of something you never needed in the first place. The Pennsylvania experience sucks.

In terms of the multi-billion dollar Superfund, save the money. These polluters were not stupid. They dumped the stuff where it won't be noticed. Zinc makes zippers. I'd rather have the zippers. People of Pennsylvania! This is America! No American has to live in Pennsylvania. Pack your stuff. On second thought, leave your stuff. Escape. We will take you in.

In Georgia, I have known tons of Pennsylvanians who have moved south. I have known only one—a dear friend—who moved back. I love him to death, but there must have been a forceps accident. Sorry Mike.

E-mail #6–Map Marker #36

No more twenties, no more basements

Delaware Water Gap is a nice little place.

The Presbyterian Church has a hiker's center. Across the street is a hiker's café. Its name is Trail's End.

Unfortunately, Pennsylvania has a habit of restaurants being closed on Mondays, most Tuesdays, and many Wednesdays. This is Tuesday. The Trail's End is closed.

I see some friends at the center, but I don't stay there. As I approached the town, I passed a section hiker. He said it smells and is in the basement of the church, and is dark and depressing. While it would be great for a broke hiker, he said, if you can afford a few bucks, stay at the country club. They have cheap, plain, but clean rooms and it sits in a gorgeous valley surrounded by the Appalachian Mountains. So I bunk in at the Delaware Water Gap Country Club. It is close to the hiker's center, so I go down for a visit. *Birdnut* is in an old La-Z-Boy chair, and he looks as exhausted as the old chair. He hiked with some young guys who burn up the trail. Often doing 20s several days in a row. Birdnut is a great hiker, but is closer to my age and linking up 20s puts much wear and tear on the body. So in this dark room, reclined and staring at the ceiling which is quite low, Birdnut says, "Bearfoot, no more 20s, no more basements. No more 20s, no more basements..." This goes on a bit too long.

I also catch up with *Wanderer*. Wanderer has had a moment of fame. A television crew waiting at the Trail Head interviews him as he comes out of the Pennsylvania mountains. It's a relatively long interview, but on television that afternoon, they use only 15 seconds of it.

They chose a portion where Wanderer is talking about the rocks. He is from one of those places up north where they talk funny. You know, like Fargo. He keeps saying raacks. "The raacks are brutal." Unshaven, thin, his eyes bulging out, and unwashed,

Wanderer, who is a really good guy, looked and sounded deranged. "The raacks are brutal, the raacks are brutal." Worse yet the sun was in his eyes, and the reporter couldn't understand him. All squinty, Wanderer kept saying over and over, "The raacks, the raacks."

The next spot on the news was about some new contagious disease that causes brain damage. I don't think this was an accident; more like a segue.

When we move into New Jersey tomorrow, we have two more days of rocks. New Jersey, while short, only 45 miles, is diverse. Rocks to begin with, then swamps, pastures, and then some old style mountain trails. Then New York.

Pennsylvania is supposedly really going to heat up next week. I am leaving just in time. I never saw an air conditioner in Duncannon or Port Clinton. I can't think of anything less to look forward to than overheated Pennsylvanians.

I thought about easing up a bit on Pennsylvania, and Pennsylvanians. Maybe even rewriting a bit. I thought about it.

Nah.

By the way, what's with those ugly uniforms Penn State wears? What's that all about?

E-mail #7

A hiss from above

Not long ago, some archeologists asked some interesting questions about an area in South America that is near the headwaters of the Amazon. Why are some of the lakes in these headwaters square? Why are some of the canals that connect these square lakes laser straight? Nature doesn't work in straight lines.

Satellite infrared pictures showed terraced agriculture of thousands of acres. This land is in the largest swamp in the world, much bigger than Montana and sparsely populated. This level of sophisticated agriculture once supported 70 to 80 million people.

Just in the past 30 years, these facts have become agreed upon. This massive civilization was advanced and sophisticated. Probably more advanced than Egypt during the same period, about 7,000 years ago. Now this civilization has almost totally disappeared. It is the greatest mystery of prehistoric civilization collapse, or was it genocide? And because the area is under water, it is next to impossible to study.

What happened to these people? Why do we know nothing about them? What wiped them out?

I hike alone, I like it that way. This is what I am thinking about when I am quickly brought back to the here and now.

I hear a loud hiss from above me. It scares the hell out of me, and I jump forward. I look back into the branches above. I cannot find the source. The hissing grows louder.

As I listen more carefully, it isn't a hiss at all, it is a rattle. It isn't from above, but below. The sound is bouncing off the canopy of trees. I look back down the Trail, where I just came from, and there coiled, looking at me is a mature rattlesnake. He is making it clear that I am not to return that way. My foot could not have missed him—if it did—by three inches.

I need to quit thinking about ancient civilizations, and keep my mind on the hike.

E-mail #8

New Jersey/New York

New Jersey, to begin with, is just a new name for Pennsylvania. Rocky, and hard hiking.

Then the Trail turns hard right and goes into low country. There is a long series of boards that are nailed onto perpendicular logs. When you step on them, the logs squish down into the swamp and the boards end about a half-a-yard apart from each other. So you jump from one board to the next. There is one section where there is actually a new board sidewalk that goes on for the better part of a mile. This was a good idea in this particular place; however, they forgot about kids and their bicycles. This has become a gathering place for pre-teenagers. They'll have to come up with some speed breakers or something to keep the kids from killing hikers.

There is a lot of wet and messiness in this low country. But the hiking is not hard. You can make some miles. It is hot, but not very hot. This section will be hell when it gets into July and August.

This part of the Trail is on the New York/New Jersey border. It's onion country. And

I smell it for miles. People brag about their black dirt, and onions. They stop bragging when I ask them if they have ever heard of Georgia Vidalia onions.

My new friend, *Rookie*, got me today. I'm hiking, and I keep hearing noises to my right. It makes me nervous after the close encounter with the rattlesnake. I keep jumping into the bog on my left.

Rookie was quietly behind me, chucking rocks into the woods, fairly close to me. He knew about my close encounter. When I finally realized he was behind me, he broke out laughing. "Got snakes on your mind, Bearfoot?"

Rookie lives in New Jersey. His wife is picking him up; he will stay at home for a while. He will miss some days and collect some zeros. But he will catch up, because he is one of those guys who can burn up the trail. Not only can he do multiple 20s, he is rumored to have done an unheard of 30. For me to do a 30, I would have to hike at my best speed for 15 hours. His best friend, Birdnut, will really miss him. And so will I.

E-mail #9–Map Marker #38

New York must have heard how much we hate Pennsylvania. Good ole' New York. Never wanting to come in second, in anything...

The first few miles of New York are painful, difficult, and yes, rocky. But New York is different. It has different kinds of rocks. They are like massive rock bubbles on top of the Bellvale Mountains. Up you go, often hand over hand. Down fast into the forest. Back up again, back on a bubble. Over and over. To my right, I catch a glimpse of Greenwood Lake. It is very hot today—the lake, though far below, looks so cool.

I cross a highway where my trail book tells me there is a terrific deli just a mile west. I take the detour. It is closed; shit! Two miles, one hour of hiking, wasted. Back to the Trail, back up to the bubbles. I get another view of the lake.

A sailboat is catching some breeze. We could use some of that up here.

I do hope there is more to New York than this.

E-mail #10

So far, it looks like the Tennessee PUD-master was promoted to New York.

E-mail #11–Map Marker #39

The AT moves into Bear Mountain/Harriman State Park. This park, once beautiful beyond description, is overwhelmed. Greater New York City has crept through the Hudson Valley, up the spectacular Hudson River, and into this area.

It's nobody's fault really. There are simply too many feet perched on this planet.

The Harriman family founded the park, giving the land and building the bridge (which made the land too easily accessible to the city). The family preserved the property for the future. Catch the park on a winter day, maybe a Tuesday when few are there, and you can see what their vision was.

But any other time—as I said—this place is overwhelmed.

I can't wait to get out of here. Let's head north—fast.

E-mail #12

The lemon squeezer. It won't get me.

It does.

Both knees and my back are scraped raw. I get squeezed. You hike between two high rock walls that get closer and closer together. Finally, they are inches apart. But with some nimbleness, you can jump up on a ledge and out. I am not nimble enough. I am stuck in the air with my legs dangling. Finally I push myself up enough to get a foothold.

The Observatory on top of Bear Mountain has a zillion steps. They force me to drag my raggedy ass up the mountain, and then they think I want to climb steps?!

What's wrong with these people?

The next day, across the bridge and on the northeast side of the Hudson River, I hear loud rumbling, and I think we are in for some serious thunderstorms. But soon it is clear that what I am hearing is artillery. West Point—the military academy—is a few miles up the Hudson. Our young military leaders of tomorrow are learning to lob shells.

Is this a military tactic of today? Aren't artillery shells obsolete? Anyway, they keep booming away all morning. This area is populated densely, but West Point was here first. I guess as people move in, listening to artillery is like living next to an airport.

June and New York are running out at the same time. I was looking forward to New York, but now I have Connecticut in my sites. And besides, New York is kind of blah.

I hear Kent is neat, where we do some river bank walking. And Connecticut has actual in-use covered bridges. Why is the future consistently more attractive than the present?

E-mail #13–Map Marker #40

I thank New York for its role in getting the AT started. In 1928, it was the first section completed and in operation. The potential beauty of the area is not lost on me.

The Harriman Bridge, the valley vaulting from the river, the monasteries perched on the cliff tops. It is quite a picturesque area. But it truly is overwhelmed each day by thousands of New Yorkers seeking solitude. All together. In the thousands. Get it?

This is also the lowest point in the Appalachian Mountains, and therefore, the Appalachian Trail. It's as close to sea level as we get. 125 feet.

But the AT quickly solves this problem, pushing us to more than 3,000 feet in Massachusetts and 6,000 feet in New Hampshire.

There is also a sad, sad zoo here. The less said about it the better.

I am in Pawling, New York, tonight and soon I will cross into Connecticut either Saturday or Sunday. Pawling has had, and still has, some interesting citizens: Edward R. Murrow, James Earl Jones, Mary Tyler Moore, writers, poets, and other New Yorkers who seek a quieter spot for part of their life. Good choice.

E-mail #14

I haven't forgotten, why did I do this?

I almost have my mind around it.

E-mail #15–Map Marker #41

What Class am I?

The Appalachian Trail has its own railroad station. It is just about on the New York/ Connecticut line. It operates only on weekends and, I think, it only stops a couple of times on those days. But the fare to New York City is mega-cheap, under $20 round trip.

I'm kinda proud of our station, and I hope it doesn't get whacked by the Amtrak crisis.

A physical update: Pennsylvania left its signature. My left knee hurts all the time. But the dart doesn't shoot me anymore. So on balance, it's better. I have lost three and one-half toe nails, and others have gone black. I learned that some black toenails are blisters under the nail. Yuck.

A new problem is my right Achilles. It has started communicating with me. The neuroma has leveled off, and is no worse. The back is still hanging in there. This, by itself, is a miracle. Those of you who have lived with me and all my back pain must be shaking your head in wonder.

I certainly am.

There are some internal things going on that I'll have to get someone to cruise through when I get back.

All in all, I'm holding my own.

I learned early that few of the self-abusers are making the cut. The bullet hikers and the ones who never come to town, the ones who never take a zero. It seems you just have to take a break, and those who don't are little-by-little leaving the Trail. They burn out. The folks who are still with me come in classes.

Class I: Tough Sumbitches. Just plain tough. I really respect them, but they are generally unpleasant people. They are older—mid-40s to mid-60s—they can handle hardship. And they really don't expect things to get better. Life sucks, then you die. But goddamit, they aren't going to go without a fight. Who knows why they are here? More misery, I guess.

Class II: The Adventurer. Usually younger and broke, these are the true spirit of the Trail. Some of the adventurers are seeking something lost. They often don't even know what that is. The non-young adventurers are similar to these—just not broke. I probably fall into this class.

Class III: The Check-Mark Group. The AT is on their list of life experiences, and they come to check it off. Real hikers who like to hike are often in this category. If you're a real hiker, have you done the AT? If the answer is yes—you are for real. Probably and most importantly to yourself.

All three classes have things in common. We are all know-it-alls. We all know everything. Our equipment is the right equipment. Our hiking strategy is the right strategy. What we eat, when, and how much is always perfectly correct. When it comes to thru-hiking, you are alone with many hard decisions. You better have confidence in yourself, so being a know-it-all isn't altogether a bad thing. Will that old bridge hold my weight? It is me who will fall forty feet if it doesn't, so it is me who is going to decide.

We also don't much give a shit if we are agreed with. This attitude can easily end a disagreement. Instead of getting bogged down with an argument, you pick up your pack and say, "See you down the Trail." And there you go, doing exactly what you want to do, how you want to do it, pretty much 24 hours a day.

We have in common the hike. The hard trails are hard. We don't play with that. Also we agree on what a thru-hiker is. You walk it all. How you go about that is up to you. No one questions it. If you skip stuff, and don't make it up, you are section-hiking not thru-hiking.

We share information. Particularly what we know about what is in front of us. We also share our hiking goals. Short-term, what we plan on doing today, and long-term, all the way through to Katahdin. This is helpful, because someone may know something important. Big and little things from dangerous places ahead on the trail, to what works against gnats, mosquitoes and other varmints. I notice those who don't share, aren't shared with and often aren't with us anymore.

We are really coming to the demarcation point. Our numbers are greatly reduced. We see a lot more section-hikers and day-hikers than we see thru-hikers. I will sometimes go a couple of days without seeing a thru-hiker. And that may continue until I come to a town or a village where we all collect.

We share a common feeling about our stuff. Our stuff is our stuff and we might give you some of it, but don't ask for it.

I have found very few thru-hikers who are not smart. I could write 100 pages on this. These folks are very smart in fact. Smart enough to the point of being a pain in the ass. To prove my point, lots of doctors are thru-hikers.

I am sure there is more we thru-hikers have in common, but I am sleepy. I am two-thirds through. I am exhausted in every way. These past few weeks have been a real chore. I must get my spirit back and up.

David and Nancy will visit in two weeks, I can't wait.

I miss my leather chair and that rare moment when Sapelo jumps up and puts her head on my leg and dozes. When she does this, I freeze, because I don't want her to leave.

I miss the guys and golf. Golf is just an excuse so we can love each other in that bizarre male way.

I miss a car. God, how I miss a car.

I miss those I love so much.

I can't carry on like this any further. Connecticut, Massachusetts, Vermont, New Hampshire, and Maine are ahead of me, and I can't wimp out now.

So stop whining.

E-mail #16–Map Marker #42

An ATM next to a hand-pump fountain

Connecticut has been a treat. It is very pretty. Fairly mild as hikes go. I stayed in Kent at a bed & breakfast and slack-packed so I could hang out a bit. By continuing to hike, I don't lose miles, but by slack-packing and coming back at night, I taste the culture and have a sense of place.

Connecticut is in a cultural clash. Their quality of life, which is fabulous, is funded by outsiders. These outsiders moved in because of that quality of life. Other outsiders are visitors and tourists. So the visitors visit for the quaintness, which is the essence of New England. When they move in, they want the conveniences they had back home. They aren't tourists anymore; they are residents. They pay taxes, they vote, and help raise property values. Locals want the money the new residents and tourists bring, because family farming is dead. But they want to preserve the agricultural culture. Preserve the quaintness. So heritage is under attack by this cultural collision.

While it is evident, it also works in a messy kind of way. The best example I can give you is the hand-pumped well-water drinking fountain I saw next to an ATM.

I like New England. Its roots are country, and I understand country.

Hikers always find the best and cheapest breakfast spot. In Kent, that is Caralee's. Even at Caralee's it isn't that cheap. Nothing is cheap in Kent. My friends pitch tents in backyards or hitch in a mile and a half from a shelter because the lodging is so expensive.

We get into this discussion and we decide that hikers are just long distance street people.

Think about it.

We stink. We sleep on the ground. When we get cold, we put on all we have in layers. Our gloves have holes in the tips of the fingers. We carry all we have with us. We will eat what other folks have thrown away. We live on the street or the Trail. And when the weather gets bad, we go to shelters others have provided for us.

We are just long distance street people.

Part of the hike today was five miles along the Housatonic River. It was a hot day. I came up on a bunch of thru-hikers in the river. It was so much fun sitting on the bank watching them. They never knew I was there. The current was strong and as they played they were gradually washed down stream. They were at least one-half mile away from their backpacks, and getting farther.

I chuckled, and after depositing a few pet rocks in their packs, I got up and went on.

The Fourth of July is in three days; I think I'll find somewhere to settle in. Maybe some place that has fireworks.

E-mail #17–Map Markers #43–44

It is hot.

It is the hottest I have ever hiked. The heat index is well over 100. Temperatures in the mid-90s; same kind of numbers for the humidity. Inhaling is like breathing soup.

The bugs love it. They are all over me. I move as best I can because to stop gives them an opportunity to land and begin feasting on me. Bugs are a major factor on the trail, and dictate much of our behavior.

Southbounders usually wait until June to leave from Maine due to the black flies. This winged hell peaks in May—between Mother's Day and Father's Day. They fly in a swarm the size of a basketball, and they love to have a human head in the center. They will enter your nose, mouth, ears or any other orifice. And they bite until you bleed. I hope I never experience them.

Southbounders wear funny hats that are nets, and wear long sleeves until they reach New Hampshire. I mention this because I may have passed my first southbound thru-hiker. To be this far south, he must have left in May. Black fly season. He blew past me, he was tough, fast, and my antenna said "thru-hiker."

As soon as I passed him, I shouted a question, "Where are you from?"

"Maine." He shouted back. As he was disappearing over an embankment, I tried one more question, "Where are you going?"

Did I hear him say Georgia?

April's family comes to hike with her a few days.

Bad choice of days. This is not a time for out-of-shape hiking.

I come to Prospect Mountain shortly after Falls Village. This is a true test of the AT, even if it isn't so hot. Megan, April's mother, is sitting on a rock one-fourth the way up the mountain. Exhausted in the heat. After chatting with her a while, I move on up the mountain. Her father found his rock halfway up the mountain. Also, not looking so good. Their 11-year-old black lab, Aurora Borealis, is with him. I give her some handfuls of water, which she appreciates, but she keeps whining and looking downhill, worried about Megan.

Aurora looks okay, but a bit strange, her coat is all tufted up and mangled. I move on and found April on the top of the mountain sitting and waiting. I mention Aurora and she explains. They had done an amateur job of shearing Aurora last night because of the heat. I told April to relax; it would be awhile before she will see her folks.

I head down the other side. Halfway down the mountain, lying in the grass, is April's little brother. I'd been told he is a rocket, an extremely fast hiker. At home he is a state champion marathon runner. We chat a bit, then he curls up to take a nap. I decide not to warn him about ticks and Lymes disease. First of all, he is a teenager and won't listen, and secondly, April will check him over tonight. I finish the mountain.

The AT skirts Salisbury and I need provisions and a break, so I stick my thumb out. First vehicle picks me up! The first! A furniture truck. When he drops me at a motel, he says, "I wish I was doing what you are doing."

I said, "Well, I'm leaving at 8 a.m. tomorrow, be here, and we'll go."

When I walk into the motel lobby, I look back, he hasn't pulled away yet.

What am I going to do if he is here?

Two neat things and one shitty thing happened on the hike today.

First I came upon a platform at the top of the mountain, but it wasn't level. It tilted down the hill. It took a minute, then I knew. This was a hang-glider's take-off platform. All the trees had been cleared by the hang-gliders who owned or leased this property, all the way to the valley, hundreds of feet below.

This gave hikers an unbelievable view.

Secondly, down below was a racecourse. Cars were moving around the course at high speeds. It was so interesting to see them do a power slide through a corner and hear the screech of their tires a few seconds later. Speed of light, much faster than the speed of sound.

Moving on, I finally cross and reach the other side of today's mountain. At this point, I encounter the nastiest man alive. He owns a filling station on the AT, and he and his dog want to make it clear he wants your money, but he hates you. And hates everyone else for that matter.

On the door, a sign reads, "Directions $2, or I will sell you a map. This is a business, not a information booth." I wanted to tell him that the third word from the end should be "an" rather than "a" but decided against it. I buy two Cokes but get two 7-Ups. I am insulted eight times—I counted. One of the 7-Ups is warm and one was cold. I open the warm one and pour it out, I didn't want him to sell it again to one of my colleagues. I drank the other one.

The AT did a big circle around a cornfield and came out on the other side of his station. Even the ATC wouldn't go in front of his place. This is truly a guy who is wasting the world's oxygen.

The good guys have outnumbered the bad guys to an extraordinary extent on this trip. But this guy deserves special notice. The notice would say, "Just outside Falls Village, across the bridge from the high school, resides the nastiest man alive."

A twister needs to drop his ass in Oz.

E-mail #18–Map Marker #45

What is a Shaker?

I really don't know what the Shaker community is all about. I know they live together in villages, and men and women live in separate buildings; or at least they did. I also know they construct splendid furniture of the simplest design.

Here in the Berkshires, architecture is influenced by this Shaker simplicity. This is where I am, in the Berkshires, which are as pretty a section of our country as there is. Western Massachusetts. Gently rolling mountains, long meadows with lovely architecture, with a great deal of homeowner pride.

Massachusetts gets lost between Connecticut and Vermont in the trail books. And it starts out badly after Bear Mountain (a different Bear Mountain from the one in New York). But just like Bostonians, it's rough to begin with, but there's gentleness inside.

Massachusetts is every bit Connecticut's equal.

There is a tiny community on the Massachusetts Trail named Tyringham. It should be on a stamp. Farmhouses, family parks, pretty bed and breakfasts, a rock post office, just right. Norman Rockwell's spirit is nearby, you can just feel him.

The Shaker village is nearby and influences the architecture. I would love to visit that village, maybe next time. I should move on.

Because of my section links, I don't shelter at Upper Goose Pond Cabin. This place is talked about often on the Trail. It sits on a Berkshire pond; the cabin has a fireplace, bunks, covered porch, canoes, and swimming. A great place to take a zero.

But it is almost a mile off the Trail, and I will take at least one zero soon when David, Nancy, and Dana visit. So I don't stop. Yet I think about it, and I'm sure many of my buddies are there. The stories must be flying

Have fun y'all.

If you guys want to think about it while you're swimming; 1,530 miles complete. 639 miles to go.

E-mail #19–Map Marker #46

There was a section back in Tennessee I think, where the red spruce took over a mountaintop, and I got lost several times in the trees and fog. As I recall, I called it an Ichabod Crane feeling. That night, I looked it up in my hiker's guide, and it said we wouldn't see this type of forest again until the Berkshires.

Well here I am, and here it is. Amazing.

Another amazing thing happened, I ended one map today and the next map starts 19 miles away. 19 miles are missing. If I were Eric the Red, the real discoverer of America, I would assume this is where the world ends, and I will fall off the edge.

If you hear from me again, it was just a printing error.

E-mail #20–Map Marker #47

A Havanese, just like Tallulah

It was not a printing error. It was my error. I did not turn the map over. AT maps are not uniform. They have different formats for different sections of the Trail. It takes a while to get used to a new set of maps. This section prints on both sides. I figured it out, I'm a smart guy.

I am moving quickly through Massachusetts. Dalton, last night; Bascom's Lodge tonight. A 20 and an 18. I am 10 miles from the Vermont line. I plan to come home the first full week in August for at least four days. At my present hiking rate, I'll be through Vermont and New Hampshire by then.

Most importantly I'll be through the Whites. The Whites and the Smokies are the most anticipated, respected, and dreaded sections of the AT. The Whites have brutal ups and downs; they ascend above tree line and have dangerous, unpredictable weather.

The worst weather on the planet has been recorded on Mount Washington. The highest on-land wind ever recorded was here; 231 miles per hour. Mount Washington has never recorded a temperature above 75 degrees. Sleet is common every month of the year. Dana is delivering my winter gear, strange for July, but people die on these mountains every year.

Within the Whites, most individual mountains are named for presidents. So this section of the White Mountains is called the Presidentials. While Mount Washington is the tallest and the worst, all these guys are nasty. Jefferson, Adams, Garfield. All of them.

My guess is, I'll enter the Whites around the 24th of July. For now, I will finish Massachusetts and enjoy Vermont.

Today, there is smoke all through Massachusetts due to wildfires in Canada. The wind pushed the smoke into New England. I have a 3,000-foot up today, and I am puffing and sucking in smoke. Jesus, how can anyone voluntarily do this to their lungs with cigarettes? I can feel my lungs try to reject this stuff with every breath.

Yesterday a spiritual event occurred.

The Trail between Upper Goose Pond and Dalton is interesting and rather flat. It goes by a number of ponds created by glaciers, with walking boards over swamps and bogs. Several gravel roads enter the area. Roads, flat, and interesting things to see. A perfect section for day hikers. And because it is a weekend day, I pass many. They bring their dogs. Folks never leash their dogs on the Trail, and they should not in my opinion. If they are not dangerous, let them run.

I always welcome meeting a dog. When I see one on the Trail, I know his day hiking group is close behind. I take a few seconds with them first to scratch their ears and say a few words.

Yesterday, I stopped in my tracks; two little dogs were leading this day-hiking group. They were Havanese. Sassafras and Tallulah Havanese. They are also known as Bichon Havanais or Havana Silk Dog. It is so rare to see these dogs, much less on the Appalachian Trail.

The girls who owned them had actually brought them from Cuba. One dog is the mother; the son was brought into the U.S. in the mother's stomach. I really enjoyed these two little guys, and somehow felt better after they departed. In fact, I moved forward with a smile on my face.

Next came the Cookie Lady.

Marilyn Wiley has been baking cookies for AT hikers for 15 years. She lives in the middle of a blueberry patch, a big one. She is an official stop on the AT and appears as such in all the AT literature. Camp out in the yard. If she goes to town, jump in the car. Maybe she'll even let you pick some berries.

And, of course, help yourself to her fresh, warm cookies.

One of the best things is her cool clean well water.

Marilyn is the keeper of the AT flame as far as I am concerned.

E-mail #21

Two pretty blue eyes

From Mount Greylock, I go down the mountains through a little town, North Adams, and back up. Just before I start ascending, I remember I have not filled my water bladder for a while. I pass one of the last houses and spot the water spigot on the side.

Very quietly, I tiptoe around the house, take off my backpack, get out my water bladder, remove the garden hose from the spigot, and start filling up. Not six inches from my face was a window. I don't notice at first, but it is open, and on the other side of the screen, just a couple of inches away are two pretty blue eyes. A little girl is watching me.

I whisper, "Can I borrow some water?"

She nods.

I finish, reattach the hose, and move up into the woods. I don't look back.

E-mail #22–Map Marker #48

Look out for those raacks!

I am officially in Vermont. After this state, two more to go. Last night, I sheltered about 17 miles from Greylock. Because I knew the Vermont line was 10 miles from Greylock, and I had hiked 17, I was seven miles into Vermont. It was a tough 17, the smoke was still in the air and I was dragging ass for some reason. I was anxious to get into my sleeping bag.

It was getting dark. There were two section-hikers and me. They had blisters. Unfortunately, I am an expert. So after much advice and first-aid, we bedded down. Then we heard a late comer stomping down the shelter trail. He was talking to himself. I know that voice.

As he made the turn, I said, "Look out for those raacks, they are brutal!"

"Bearfoot!" Wanderer said, laughing.

We caught up with the news; it was great to see him.

The next day I had to buy some stuff so when I got to Vermont Highway 9, I hitched into Bennington. I had been there before. Vermont looks like a good place to live. At least the southern half.

I would like to see the Northern Kingdom. But because the AT turns east halfway up into Vermont, we don't see the very northern part which is known as the Northern Kingdom. Many people I respect would say there is not a prettier spot in America.

The Trail in Vermont has been unpleasant. Not enjoyable. There was one spot though, where I was hiking through acres of ferns, nothing else, just ferns. That was nice.

I hope, like Massachusetts, that Vermont gets better as we move north.

E-mail #23

Shoe-Goo

Shoe-Goo does not adhere to—what? First of all, those of you who don't know what Shoe-Goo is, you should be ashamed of yourselves. You have been raised in a much too pampered and affluent childhood.

Shoe-Goo holds together shoes that are falling apart. I buy it by the carton. It is this gooey stuff that comes out of a toothpaste-like tube, and dries rubbery. My hiking shoes are constantly falling apart. Lately, it's been in multiple spots that adjoin each other. So the Shoe-Goo is in contact with itself.

Shoe-Goo does not adhere to Shoe-Goo. I never knew this. I have a problem. I'm not sure my shoes will survive the Whites. But once I leave Hanover, it will be too late to change. These are my fourth pair.

I like my shoes. The Whites are not a good place to be breaking in new ones. Hmmmm…

E-mail #24–Map Markers #49, 50, 51

A character update

Pipe Wrench is the greatest. He is so approachable. Just plain nice. Considerate and respectful, I see him a lot and I'm always glad. He is thin, close shaven, and a hell of a hiker. Fast—real fast. He beats me to the same destination by hours. The only reason I ever catch him is that he takes zeros. I seldom do. Pipe Wrench likes to pair up or hike with a group. This, I think, is because of his natural friendliness. But groups are hard to keep going. There is always one that needs to stop for something.

Tim and *Ruth*. I can't ever remember their Trail names (*Cash* and *Dragonfly*), and somehow I learned their real names and it stuck. Tim has movie star looks, even wet and muddy at the end of the day. He is a genuinely happy person, and sees so much good around him. He is very smart.

Ruth is rock solid. She is surely everyone's best friend back home. Great, positive attitude, cute—not gorgeous but pretty, she has a strong hiker's body—which looks good on a woman. They are engaged. They will be terrific parents. Their kids—yet unborn—will be blessed.

Wizard, I can't connect with. He has a bit of Turkey Bacon in him, less asshole quotient, but enough.

Scout, the only glamorous female hiker I've seen, has left the Trail. She has some Asian in her DNA that gives her a sense of mystery. I like her a lot, but she is tough, not to be trifled with.

Turkey Bacon is a no show. Either he dropped out after Trail Days, or he is way back.

I am told *Gunslinger* and *Sparrow* ran out of money and went home. They were ready. I don't think the money had much to do with it. A big hint was when they showed up with a puppy they carried on the Trail. Give me a break, they were ready to go home.

Rawhide is a no show. Once he was up ahead, but no one sees him in the registers anymore.

Panama is a new friend. He and Pipe Wrench have paired up. He wears a Panama hat naturally. Never a shirt when he hikes. A very good chap. He is a good partner to Pipe Wrench. Two quality guys.

The Mass Four left the Trail for a while, but they are back. I hear their mood is low and a lot of pressure is on Devin to keep their spirits up.

The Four Horsemen, a group of wild college kids who found themselves together in Virginia, broke up, and I am only sure that *Huck*, their leader, is still moving. *Christopher Robbin*, who would have been a Fifth Horsemen had he met them earlier, is doing well, about a week ahead of me.

Wanderer—is well—Wanderer. Doing great. Mood great. Knocking out 20s. What a tough dude.

The *Flying Pork Chop* is still finding nice things to say about something everyday. His entries in the registers are a delight. It appears he will meet his August 15 deadline in time for his wedding.

Probably my favorite friend on the Trail now is Pipe Wrench, but close second to him is *Birdnut*. I miss Jeff and Stone who have both moved on, but Birdnut is a different kind of friend and a good one. Birdnut and I don't see each other often, but when we do there's a kinship.

He's the type of person everyone trusts. A very hard working hiker. The first to leave camp every morning. Dogged and disciplined. He goes at it. He puts in the days and, each day, he puts in the miles. And he really is a bird nut. He knows all about them. He doesn't talk to me much about birds, I think because he sees my eyes glaze over whenever he tries. I really try to look interested, but...

He is distancing himself from me. When he gets to two days, he will be gone, and I will miss seeing him. He is short, bearded and always neat. He doesn't smile easily, but when he does it is delightful. Everything in his face smiles. When he smiles, everyone around him smiles. I love the guy, and don't have a clue how to get in touch with him when all this is over.

Bearfoot is looking forward to the Whites, believe it or not. They are unique. My spirits are fine, but this has not gotten any easier. My pack is not any lighter. And loneliness is enclosing me like a vice. The Trail is more rugged. Harder to navigate as we walk on. It is quite narrow—18 inches at times with ground cover growing over. Because of this, I often don't know where my foot will land. All this is because the Trail is less traveled in the far north.

I have slowed down, not for any reason but that it is harder. A rugged trail, less visibility, and many steep ups and downs.

The only way I can do a 20 is to hike 10 hours. While this is enormously difficult, the one thing in my favor is daylight. I have 14–15 hours of daylight.

That will change soon, so I must press on.

I finally fell in love with Vermont, not the Trail so much as the villages. Highway 7 parallels the AT and there are easy hitches into Bennigton and Manchester.

Many of my friends had collected in Manchester to re-provision. We had Mexican food in this extremely civilized place. We were kept outside and off by ourselves by the proprietor. There we were—*Jitterbug*, *Presto*, Cash, Dragonfly, Panama, Pipe Wrench, and Bearfoot.

Dana and my good friends, David and Nancy Stonecipher visited so I took a full zero here.

We were told the wilderness would quickly return in a drastic fashion, and that this civilized portion of the Trail will end. And it did, almost as soon as we entered New Hampshire, so we enjoy our short stay in Manchester.

But we had our graduation party at the Inn at Long Trail in Killington two days later.

Hard hiking got me here in the dark, and I was surprised to see everyone again. There must have been 20 thru-hikers drinking beer and eating hamburgers. All of the above plus Mr. Wizard, April, and a few others I didn't know. I had hiked all day and saw no one. I arrived at this traditional stopping place, and there they all were, way ahead of me in the celebration, but I caught up.

I hiked the next day with six or seven people, which was very unusual for me. I always preferred hiking alone, and everyone knew that. We arrived at our pre-planned shelter and found it over-filled by a weekend camping group.

There we were, plus all of them. I felt claustrophobic. My group started to set up their tents, and I just stood there. These were my friends, but I couldn't stay tonight. April and Pipe Wrench could tell.

"See you down the Trail?" April said.

I smiled at her. "Yeah."

I turned and continued north. A downpour hit. I was soaked, and I had a smile on my face.

The next day I bushwhacked my way to a dirt road, and some fishermen on four-wheelers got me to a paved road where I could hitch to Woodstock. I wanted to see this place, and I am glad I did. It may be the prettiest village in America.

E-mail #25

A needle in a haystack has much better odds than this.

A month or so ago, Pipe Wrench needed to go to D.C. for a wedding. He planned to catch the railroad when he reached Harper's Ferry.

As he crossed the Harper's Ferry Bridge entering the city, he met up with a guy who was doing some conditioning hiking, preparing to be an A.T. Southbounder. He said his Trail name would be *Play-doh*.

Play-doh, coincidentally, lived just a mile or so from where Pipe Wrench needed to go for this wedding, so he gave Pipe Wrench a ride and they became friends.

Fast forward to today. Mid-July, West Hartford, Vermont.

We don't see much of West Hartford. We cross the White River on a pretty, old iron bridge and then we reenter the woods on the east side. But just before we do, there is a tiny general store that makes sandwiches.

I enter the store and there sits this fellow. I don't know his name. Or anything about his background. He is the first southbound thru-hiker I have formally met, and I have a thousand questions. What a great guy. He patiently answers all my questions.

The sandwiches are terrific, not to mention the milkshakes. As we are finishing, who walks in but Pipe Wrench? "Play-doh! Bearfoot." He says.

There are over 2,000 miles on the AT. What are the chances of three hikers walking in different directions, coming together in this one spot? My first real Southbounder, my friend Pipe Wrench, a Northbounder, runs into his friend, a Southbounder, who is now my friend ... Never mind.

E-mail #26–Map Marker #52

Elm Street

Several miles after West Hartford, the Trail deposits us on Elm Street in Norwich, Vermont. Elm Street is a residential street like thousands in the U.S. Lovely homes, nice folks who choose to share their street with smelly hikers. A couple of citizens wave at me as I pass. A lady watering her flowers gives me a drink from her hose.

Unlike Duncannon, Pennsylvania, which rerouted the AT away from their beautiful main street (every other storefront is plywood rather than glass). Elm Street is proud of the AT and what it stands for.

Go figure.

Elm Street gives way; we cross a bridge, this time the New Hampshire River, and we are in Hanover, the home of Dartmouth College, and I enter the next to the last state of my journey.

I love college towns. I love them. They are the right blend of everything a town should be. Everyone should live in one, but if they did, it would be a city, and cities suck.

E-mail #27–Map Marker #53

"I bet you folks don't see many smelly, broke Appalachian hikers in here."

New Hampshire, the home of the Whites. On July 24th, I will enter the White Mountains. But for now, I am in Hanover, or nearly. I walk up a long street to the town. The first place I see is a very upscale hotel—the Hanover Inn. I turn left at the light and arrive at Robinson Hall, which houses the Dartmouth Outing Club. They assist thru-hikers, and the Hiker Club volunteer tells me about a motel for $50 a night, two miles out of town. "You can hike it, or catch the bus in front of the hotel." Screw that, I think, and I march into the Hanover Inn. Not exactly a hiker's hostel. My treking pole tips might adhere to rock, but, I discovered, not to marble. This place is posh.

With my biggest smile, I walk up to the front desk. "I bet you folks don't see many smelly, broke Appalachian hikers in here." She burst out laughing, a good sign.

"How long have you been hiking?" she asks.
"Since February, or 1,750 miles."

"Wow."

"Do you folks have any singles left for tonight?"
"Yes, we do, they normally start at $250 per night."

I like that word normally.

"Well," I say, "some hotels have a couple of rooms for Appalachian thru-hikers. Like the White Heart Inn in Salisbury."

"How much did they charge?" And so I tell her.
"Well, we can do better than that." And she did. Forty-five bucks.

As I settle in my room, through the window I see Wanderer and Pipe Wrench waiting for the bus out on the street. I had beat the rate they would get two miles away.

I raised the window and shouted. "Hey Wanderer, look out for those raacks."

E-mail #28–Map Marker #54

Winniepesaukee

I began New Hampshire which at first was tame. I passed a little stream which had soft drinks in it. A trail angel was helping us deal with the heat.

My mind was ready to sprint for the finish line, but I didn't realize my body was shot.

George and Jane Benson, my good friends, sent me a voice mail asking me to spend some time with them at Lake Winnipesaukee, their summer home. It just seemed right. I called and accepted. At the lake, I took a full zero and a half. I fell asleep in their hammock six times. I had no idea how tired I was. Everything is stronger now.

George shuttled me from and to the Trail. He took me back to my last stopping point. I didn't know how to tell him how perfect this visit was. I didn't spend much time with him; most of the time, I was asleep.

But I think he knew.

When we reached the Trail, he walked with me into the forest for a while. I could see it in his eyes, he had a thru-hiker's spirit. We hugged and he turned around.

How can you put a value on friendship? I must be a better one when I get back.

E-mail #29–Map Markers #55

Nearing the Whites

These sections of New Hampshire are pretty. Mount Cube has beautiful views. There is one more short section before we officially enter the Whites. It is a huge camelback mountain named Moosilauke.

It is huge and very high. And very steep. It juts above the tree line, our first experience with this, and probably would be in the Presidentials except it isn't in the National Park, mostly privately owned.

It is a final and true test.

There is a hostel at the base. Hikers Welcome Hostel. Run by a couple of past thru-hikers who are experimenting with backpacks. These backpacks unfold into tents. This is really cool stuff and I think they will hit it big.

It turns out that most of my hiking buddies have collected here. Resting and preparing for the Whites.

We will spread out after this because of reservations in the White's Huts (I'll explain later). It is likely the last time I will see most of them, as I have to leave the Trail for about a week for business on the other side of the Whites.

There are about 20 of us here. 15 are friends. It is a wonderful time. There is tons of laughter.

In addition to Birdnut, Pipe Wrench, and all the others, Rookie has returned. He was the guy who was chunking rocks behind me back in New Jersey. He is a hoot, and a long distance hiker. He can nail 30s. He and Birdnut are inseparable. This is a great friendship that will last a lifetime. Two great guys.

E-mail #30–Map Markers #56–57

The Whites begin.

Mount Moosilauke is a test. It is also beautiful. It is owned by a family who donated it to Dartmouth College. Therefore, it is privately owned, but completely surrounded by The White Mountain National Forest.

Technically, therefore, it's not in the Whites.

It climbs 1,800 feet immediately in a linear mile. This is beyond brutal. Then it continues to climb until it reaches 4,800 feet. This height is just enough to poke above the tree line. Absolutely amazing. I don't know how to describe the unimpeded views, standing on top of a mountain with no vegetation.

Maybe I should be corrected. There is what's known as arctic vegetation. Sort of a moss but, other than that, rocks.

Most of the Presidential peaks are above tree line. I will be ridge walking above that line for hours.

Yesterday, I entered the "true" Whites, crawling over Kinsman Mountain to Lonesome Lake Hut.

It poured on me starting about noon. It was the most difficult hike of the trip. The terrain was tough enough. Hand over hand for much of it, and rain made it even more treacherous. The Trail was ankle deep. Added to this, the blazes stopped. For three-quarters of a mile there were no blazes. In other words, I was not being told that I was still on the Appalachian Trail.

You are instructed in all the books not to continue if you haven't seen a blaze in one-fourth of a mile.

I kept pushing it.

It got colder, wetter, and more treacherous. The thought that I would summit soon kept me going forward.

I kept looking, slipping on rocks, and moving through dangerous and monstrously steep grades.

I would hold onto trees and, many times, I would lose my footing only to save myself hanging one-handed onto a tree limb. The Trail was a water-route chute, there was really no reason for your foot ever not to slip.

Still no blazes.

Was I going up another trail? Another mountain? Was I about to get lost in the Whites in a storm? I push further.

Finally, I knew I had gone two-thirds of a mile with no blaze. Three times more than what they say is the turnaround point. I turned around. I started down.

Downhill was no easier than up.

Finally, I saw a yellow baseball cap coming up. It was *Lloyd*. I haven't spoken of Lloyd before although I've run into him several times. Lloyd is a tough, no-nonsense thru-hiker who refused to get to know any of us. No one had ever seen him smile. He had on shorts and a t-shirt. The temperatures were in the fifties. He was soaked through and through. As was I. I had returned now about one-half a mile. I told Lloyd that I had turned around.

Lloyd was insistent that this was the AT. He convinced me and I turned back up the mountain once more.

I was now doing some of the hardest hiking I had ever done for the third time. Up, down, up again.

After a half mile, Lloyd was also quite concerned about seeing no blazes. It was getting late. The weather had worsened. The wind was stronger than anything I had experienced since the Smokies. The rain was horizontal.

We stopped and pulled out my maps. We decided to go forward. Any side trail we could see on the map returned us to the AT, or intersected with a trail that did.

We were at the point where I had originally turned around. 100 yards later, it became obvious we were cresting. 100 yards after that, a blaze. We were on the AT. I had spent three hours going up and down, hand over hand, falling and slipping, because the Appalachian Mountain Club led by the ATC had chosen not to blaze the Trail.

I now had six more miles to Lonesome Lake Hut.

The ATC promises to blaze the Trail no less than every one-fourth of a mile. More so on tough terrain. Didn't happen.

Their failed responsibility created a dangerous situation. At the Hut, the talk was all about "hiking on faith" and the absence of blazes on the south side of Kinsman Mountain. Guess what? Once we crested, every damn tree and rock was blazed. North side, well blazed. South side, nada.

I was so pissed I blew up all over some nice young kid at the hut who was working for the AMC (Appalachian Mountain Club). He promised to send a message to headquarters.

I went to my bunk in the hut, and tried to see what was ruined, wet, or bleeding.

In one of my falls, my watch was grabbed by a point of a rock, and popped off. I landed in a mud pit and right in my lap, landed my busted watch. This seemed to be the only thing broken. My *Data Book*, my Trail bible, was soaked and I wasn't sure if it would be usable. I'd made a lot of small notes, precious memories, that were now lost in the runny ink. I keep my *Data Book* in the same baggie with my maps. When we lost faith and pulled out the maps, it was soaked.

Backpack and everything in it is wet. My pack cover isn't made for horizontal rain.

Ruth and Tim, or if you prefer, Dragonfly and Cash, were in the hut. They are so great, my spirits are raised.

The day of days is ended.

E-mail #31–Map Markers #58

Huts

In the Whites, a unique series of cabins exist. They are called huts. They hold between 40 and 90 people. I think there are about eight of them and they run the length of the Whites. The huts serve a hearty, if not tasty, breakfast and dinner. The bunks are comfortable with a pillow and three blankets. The bunks stack up ten high sometimes. Water, but no hot water, no showers. Lights go off about nine o'clock.

For an AT hiker, it means you can lighten your pack depending on how many huts you can reserve, which is not easy. Most huts are fully reserved months in advance.

Also, the Whites can have tough weather, especially at night. Being inside is nice when it's storming.

They are very busy. Lots of families, kids, scouts. But a good deal better than a three-sided lean-to. I had made reservations through the Whites in huts which began on the 24th at Lonesome Lake. I made and prepaid more reservations than I thought I might need which gave me some scheduling flexibility.

The next day I hiked up to Mount Lafayette and stayed overnight at the Greenleaf Hut. The view rivals any mountain view. Stunning. Today, after the rain yesterday, the atmosphere is crystal clean. We have 130 miles of visibility. The Whites give and they take away.

I hope the weather will hold until after Mount Washington in three or four more days.

The difficulty of the Whites is greater than anything on the AT. So is the beauty. New Hampshire possesses the crown jewel of U.S. mountain hiking.

E-mail #32–Map Markers #59

Thinking about Maine

Today I went over Mount Garfield. Many say the hardest stretch of the Whites. I will not argue with them. Originally, I laughed when I was told I would be exhausted and have a full day in after only 8 miles.

However, they were right. I was completely spent. Galehead Hut sits in the most private part of the Whites. The mountains circle around. There is a beautiful view of Mount Garfield. I took pictures of the Galehead Hut from the summit at Garfield, and vice-versa. I hope they both turn out.

Tomorrow, the Trail crosses the highway. If I can do 14 miles, I'll try to hitch to a small town 10 miles north, where there are some motels.

I haven't had a shower, read a paper, or had a Coke or a beer in five days. Town seems right. Sunday and Monday, I will be in the heart of the Presidentials.

Then, I will finish the Whites. Next the Mahoosucs, which are just the Whites' AKA. The Mahoosucs in Maine are hated more than the Whites. I hear it is because they abuse you just as much, but don't reward you as much. They are not as dramatic or as beautiful. They don't have ridges so you go the entire way down, hike flat a bit, and go all the way up. Bummer.

But Maine is the last state. I'll accept anything it throws at us. The average to get through the state is 20 days. The Mahoosucs first, some level going, the 100-mile wilderness, then Baxter State Park where Katahdin resides. I don't need any jinxes, so I will stop "looking ahead." Let's just get through the Presidentials.

E-mail #33

Sometimes things work out.

I had a reservation at Zealand Falls Hut, but I swallowed hard when I got there. I walked in and told the college guys that run it to cancel my reservation. I was pushing on. It was seven miles to the highway. I had no idea how hard that seven miles would be. Would I be able to find a motel? Could I get a reservation? Could I get a hitch to the motel?

Sometimes things work out!

The seven miles after Zealand Falls were the easiest in the Whites. I did it in less than three hours. There was plenty of light. The Trail ended close to a little snack bar, with great hot dogs and ice cream. It was called Willey House. It had a phone. Next to the phone was the Crawford Notch Visitor's Center that had a picture of a beautiful hotel only five miles away. I had seen this hotel's picture many times. The Mount Washington Hotel. Famous throughout the world. I called. It had a single.

E-mail #34–Map Marker #60

Mount Washington Hotel was fun and relaxing.

This hotel will celebrate its 100th anniversary Sunday.

One of the anniversary weekend events was a ride to see the bottom of the Cog.

The Cog Railroad was built 120 years ago and claims to be the oldest in the world. It climbs to the top of Mount Washington. Thru-hikers hate it.

Remember back in North Carolina when I climbed Wayah Bald? And I was so incensed because of all the civilians who had ridden up in their cars?

Over time, I realized everything on the AT is harder. I've also learned that wherever there are civilians, there are ice cream and Cokes. So we shouldn't hate civilians.

Everywhere we go, there is an easier, faster, mechanized way to get there. That is not the point. In America, wilderness is a choice. Hiking is a choice.

Maybe the Cog is targeted because it is so noisy and belches smoke. The Trail intersects with the Cog. It is a tradition that, if you are on the Trail when the Cog comes by, you moon it. The Cog operators keep rocks of coal and chunk them at the exposed fannies.

E-mail #35–Map Marker #61

Mount Washington

Behind me tonight are the Presidentials. Webster (never a president), Jackson, Eisenhower, Franklin (never a president), Washington, Clay (never a president), Jefferson, and Adams. I am in the Madison Hut. Tomorrow morning, as I move on, I will say good-bye to Madison, whose peak I am 500 feet below at this moment. Then leave the Presidentials.

Everything about the Whites is maxed. The trails are the hardest, the rocks are the worst (forget Pennsylvania), the summits are the most spectacular, the views—second to none—are awe-inspiring, the huts are the friendliest, and the lack of blazes is the most blatant. So everything is maxed. It's truly the pinnacle of the AT thru-hike.

A word or two about Mount Washington. I've had good weather for the last few days, so this mountain has been omnipresent. Anytime you choose to, from anywhere, you could look over your shoulder and there it was. You could never mistake it.

Powerful music jumps into your head whenever you look at it.

Mount Washington is named well. The granddaddy of mountains. Clingmans Dome is the tallest mountain on the AT, but it isn't a presence. Mount Washington is a presence.

You fear it. You fear its penchant for danger. You respect it. Knowing it could huff and puff and blow you off its back whenever it pleased. It is angry, and hurts—even kills—people. When you start up Mount Washington, a sign states that if you need to be rescued, either you—or your estate—will pay the tab.

Because it is above tree line, it is naked looking down on the other peaks of the Presidentials.

There is clearly a majesty one feels. I am proud to be here. The auto road and the Cog bring tourists when the weather permits. This offends some hikers, but I feel they have as much right to be here as we do.

The Whites are the defining chapter of the AT. Mount Washington is the exclamation point.

E-mail #36

The anti-climax is now the rest of the Whites, and the Mahoosucs are coming up. Then I must go home for a few days, then return to finish the balance of Maine.

It is proper that the Presidentials are near the end. A fitting, almost theatrical sequencing. When the AT was conceived, its father, Mackey, planned for the Terminus to be Mount Washington. Mainers convinced him to push on to Katahdin. I understand both points of view. But nothing I have ever seen has the majesty of the Presidentials.

I am sorry for Southbounders who rush through here. I met a group who did the entire Presidentials in one day. 19 hours of hiking. What a shame.

I will bring the ones I love back here. They must see and feel this. My hiking heart is left here, only legs remain for the finish.

E-mail #37–Map Marker #62

I made a big mistake.

I wrote about the Presidentials in the past tense, while the summit of Mount Madison was looking over my shoulder. Big mistake.

I woke up in the Madison Hut to the worst weather of the trip. Visibility was a few feet. Raining, sometimes very hard, and unbelievable winds, estimated at 40–50 miles per hour. We ate our breakfast in an eerie quiet, listening to the winds rock the hut.

Bucky, my friend from Burlington, North Carolina, skipped breakfast and headed out at 6:00 a.m. He is a slow but tenacious hiker. He puts in many miles because he hikes many hours. Bucky is in his mid-60s and has run over 100 road races. Because he has maintained his speeds, but has gotten older, he will qualify this year for the Boston Marathon.

Bucky is small. 5'9" maybe 140 pounds. I worry about him climbing to the summit of Mount Madison in this weather.

We finish breakfast. The weather is posted. It is awful. We expect the hut crews to tell us to stay put, but they don't. So we start pulling our stuff together. I go as slowly as I can, but in spite of that, I am the first to leave.

The way down is up. I have 500 feet of rock scramble to get over Madison and start down the Presidentials to Pinkham Notch.

As soon as I turn the corner of the hut, I am blown down. The first of a dozen or more falls.

I head up.

In the fog, I look for the silhouettes of the cairns.

Cairns are a pile of rocks like a small pyramid, from 3 feet to 6 feet in height. The AT blazes are painted on them because there are no trees. Above the tree line, particularly in the fog, cairns are visible as spooky images in the distance. As you get closer, if you are on the AT, you spot the blaze. Because of fog and weather, cairns are indispensable.

There is no trail. You walk on rocks, moving from cairn to cairn.

When I am on my feet, I move in this crablike walk; low, with my arms out, poles down. The wind is from the west, I am moving northeast. If I can just get over the mountain, maybe it will block some of the wind.

I give the AMC and the ATC high marks over Madison. I never lost sight of the trail. There are always cairns and enough of those are blazed.

My problems today are not man-made.

I am moving slowly. My pack gets caught in the wind and whips me around. I break one of my poles. I sit down, and in the malestrom, had to pull out my duct tape and repair it. It seems like an hour when I come upon a sign pointing back to the hut I just left. It says the Madison Hut is two-tenths of a mile away. Have I really only gone two-tenths of a mile in an hour?

Am I at the summit yet? Isn't two-tenths of a mile 500 feet? I see something blue. As I get closer, it is a person crouched in a ball on the side of the mountain. It's Bucky.

As I come to him, he has found a small indenture or hole in the rocks to hunker down in, he is stuffing his tent inside his pack. In order to hear, we have to get an inch apart.

He is okay. He has been in this place, unable to move, for an hour. Each time he tried to summit the mountain, he was blown back. He felt he simply wasn't heavy enough to fight the wind gusts that he estimated had been as much as 80 miles per hour at the summit.

His sleeping mat was jerked from his backpack by the wind and disappeared into the fog. He didn't want the same thing to happen to his tent, so he was putting it inside the backpack. He seemed ok, not delirious, which comes with hypothermia. But I disagreed with stopping and waiting; it could get worse.

I suggest we slide around the east side of the crest, keeping the mountain in front of the wind.

Staying put or sitting down was not something I was going to do. I felt it was important to keep moving no matter how slowly, as long as I was sure I was on the AT. Bucky was my friend, but I had to keep moving. I try to convince him once more.

Bucky tells me to go on, that he is going to move on too. About 20 steps later, I felt something on my right shoulder.

I look around; the wind had worked its way between my backpack and my pack cover.

A pack cover is sort of a waterproof pillowcase-looking thing that you pull over your backpack when it rains.

The second I figure out what is beating me on the shoulder, the wind rips the cover off and I watch it fly upward, billowing out, at an unbelievable rate of speed and disappearing into the fog over the abyss that the mountain cliffs create.

Watching this large black object disappear into the fog is one of the most terrifying sights I have ever beheld because I know as far as the mountain winds were concerned, the difference between me and Bucky and our gear which was being ripped off, isn't much.

Hundred mile an hour gusts are commonplace in the Whites. At one point, the wind gets so strong, that I crouch crab-style and hold the rocks with my hands and spread my legs until the wind eases a bit.

Later, I feel I am moving downward.

Then I am sure I am. I feel I am getting some blockage from the wind, and then I am sure of it.

It stopped raining some time ago, but I wasn't aware of it. Suddenly, there is total quiet and stillness. For a few seconds, the wind ceases. And I become aware that visibility must be a couple of hundred feet.

I turn around, no Bucky. I call out to him. No answer. What do I do? There are 1,200 trails in the Whites. They are constantly intersecting with the AT, and they had intersected with the Trail several times since the summit.

Also, except for blazing, the AT is not referred to on any signs. The Whites use their own trail names, arrogantly refusing to put the AT on their signposts.

We had not passed any cliffs or ravines, so I didn't think Bucky had "fallen off" anything. But he could have hunkered down again.

Visibility continues to improve and I can see well up the mountain. There is no sign of him.

Had Bucky followed me from the summit? I realize that I have not seen him or spoken to him from that point. I did not see him when my backpack cover was ripped off. He could have gone back to the hut, or taken another trail down, on purpose or by accident. I wait, then I turn and head on down. The rest of my hike down the last of the Presidentials range to Pinkham Notch is difficult but uneventful. The most difficult and dangerous trail in Georgia or North Carolina doesn't compare to the Whites in any way. As a hiker, I am redefined. I re-evaluate my day and I don't think I would have done anything differently, I feel more relieved than victorious. And I worry, where is Bucky?

Pinkham is the nerve center for the Appalachian Mountain Club. The AMC has a shuttle system that ends here. If you want to park your car, hike into the Whites, stay in a hut or two, then come down the other side; you simply find a shuttle stop and get picked up to return to your car.

Thousands of hikers enter the White Mountains every week at many different trailheads. They hike their favorite trails, which stretch over 8,000 acres of the White Mountains.

At Pinkham, a number of my hiking friends are staying at the Joe Dodge Lodge. I ask about Bucky, but no one has seen him. Some hikers who followed me from Mount Madison about an hour later, also said they had not seen him on the AT, which was the Trail they had used to get down.

Friends appear. Giggles and Highwater, the Canadian girls who should have been a week ahead of me. They were on Mount Washington today, but the winds were so bad they were brought down the auto road, and they caught the shuttle over to Pinkham. Tomorrow they will start here, and hike southward up to the crest to the summit at Mount Washington, where they left off today, and come down by hitching.

Otter is here. He is not my favorite guy, too FOS.

Otter's best buddy is the machine-gun giggler. So you can imagine what kind of personality he has. But we are all nice to Otter because his son has joined him at Pinkham to hike a few days.

E-mail #38–Map Marker #63

Gorham, the last stop before Maine

The next day is uneventful. New Hampshire's final stop is Gorham. A lot of folks slack-pack from Pinkham to Gorham, using independent shuttle drivers to carry their packs from Pinkham's Notch to some predetermined place in Gorham. Even though this section is technically still the Whites, we all feel they ended at Pinkham's Notch. Many of us know our spiritual hike is over, but the physical hike has a few more weeks.

Cash and Dragonfly are here. Dragonfly had a little pull-off-your-toenail-operation thing by a doctor here. It is good she went to a doctor. We often take these off ourselves, jerking a half lost toenail off a friend's toe lacks any sense of science. It is pretty brutal stuff. She had gone over Mount Madison with an infected foot. The pain must have been excruciating. She is quite a hiker. But she will not be hiking for a few days. Pipe Wrench is here. Panama and Wanderer are here. I saw them all and have dinner with Pipe Wrench. Looking up from my soup, I see sitting at the bar, enjoying his soup, Bucky.

I jump up!

I am so glad to see him. I thought he was okay, but it is still great to see him. We talk as old Army buddies must.

He tells me what happened after I left the summit on Mount Madison. Bucky decided to sit down for just a little bit longer, and left about 15 minutes after I did. He came directly down the AT, crossed Pinkham's Gap, and stayed in the shelter a mile on the other side.

After dinner, I walk around Gorham. They are having a musical concert in the park, which is in the center of town. It is an idyllic, small town at its best.

I buy an ice cream cone and head back to my motel room. I am conflicted, emotionally, tonight.

I am glad I'm coming home for a few days. I miss home so. But my friends are quickening the pace to get to Katahdin and finish. They are talking about crest dates in the teens. I won't be back to this spot until the 7th or so, and I don't expect to be at Katahdin until very late August or early September. I won't be with any of them at the finish. My guess is that I won't see most of them ever again.

When Pipe Wrench heads to his motel room, I say, "See you down the Trail." He doesn't turn, but he does raise his hand.

One fleeting moment

Three straight days of hard, hot hiking without a shower left me ripe. The unemployed paper worker, not only picked me up hitchhiking—when he probably shouldn't—but also went out of his way to bring me here. I wished I didn't smell so badly.

"It really isn't far." He said, pointing up a neglected road. "Go to the end of the road, turn to the left, and you'll see the landing strip."

"I can't thank you enough, please let me chip in for the gas."

He wouldn't hear of it. He smiled and tipped his Red Sox cap. The truck jerked once then moved out and soon disappeared.

It was all quiet here. And became more and more quiet as I reached the end of the road. I saw the landing strip. The mile or so of concrete runway was deserted. When the two paper plants were in full production, the airport was busy. Private planes landed and took off. My driver told me the airport even had a commercial flight once a day. All was silent now. So silent that sounds you normally never hear could clearly be heard. The light wind. A leaf skittering along the concrete in front of me on the road.

Hiking on a paved road was different. You don't look at your feet. You walk more than you hike. I hated gnarly trails, but even more, I detest hiking on paved roads. I reached the airstrip entrance. The chain link fence was open, no one was around.

What do I do now?

I walked out to the end of the runway, and I see that I am surrounded by mountains. Down past the end of the runway about 30 miles is Mount Washington. I couldn't see him now, but I knew he was there.

I slung off my backpack, pulled out the murder mystery I'd been reading, and lay down in the border grass to read. The murder mystery was mostly gone, physically gone, because as all hikers do, I threw away the pages I had read. You never carry extra weight when you're a thru-hiker.

It was hot, early August in New Hampshire. Record highs. But the sky was clear. I read on. I stunk so badly my eyes watered.

I couldn't concentrate on the book, so I lay there and did something I was incapable of doing five months ago—I did nothing. I lay there quietly looking at the clouds. Sometime later, I am not sure how much later, there was a dot in the sky. I watched as it took shape, then I could hear it. A few minutes later it passed over my head. Sleek and gleaming, it circled and lined up with the airstrip. It touched down, moving away from me. I stood up. The jet turned and headed back.

I picked up my backpack and threw it across my body with my left hand, threading my right arm through one shoulder strap. Handling a 40-pound backpack this way would have been impossible for me last Christmas. An experienced hiker will carry his backpack on one shoulder if he isn't going far, much like a golfer or a caddie might carry a golf bag. I left the grass and walked to the end of the runway.

The bill of my cap was disintegrating, it was my favorite cap, and I just wouldn't give up on it. My shorts were torn in multiple places. Neither my beard nor my hair had been trimmed in months.

There was an important meeting of a board I serve on, and I was leaving the Trail for a few days via this jet, which had landed on a deserted runway in New Hampshire. The plane taxied slowly toward me, and stopped about ten yards away. There it was, and there I was—nose to nose. The life I have chosen these past months, and the one I came from confronted each other. I had one fleeting moment when my new, strong legs were calling to me to break and run. But, of course, I didn't. The door raised, the steps descended.

"Mr. Pittard? Is that you?"

Mike, the pilot, knew me well, but he wasn't sure it was me. I smiled at him.

"I'll help you with that." Mike took my backpack. I stayed on the tarmac and made sure that it was stowed well. Mike seemed to understand and handled it with respect and gentleness. My life was in that bag. I waited until the cargo door was closed before I ascended.

"Catch the aroma, Mike?" He smiled but didn't respond. I crawled in, and sat down in too much luxury.

"We'll have you home in a couple of hours." Amazing. It took me more than five months to get here. But to get home—a couple of hours, pretty much devoid of any sense of accomplishment. We took off and flew straight over Mount Washington. Although I didn't know it at the time, a few days before, a hiker friend of mine died on that mountain.

A thought near the finish

I have boldly told my friends how tired I am of this, and how happy I will be when it is over. It is true that life without home and family is impossible for me. Dana completes me. I hope she would say the same about me. Home is where she is.

However, I am hearing some background music in my soul, and it is gaining volume. It is a melody of loss. Sad, but beautiful. A waltz of love lost. I can clearly begin to feel that I will miss this. Not the whole process—but untouchable moments.

The simplicity of life. The confidence reward of overcoming obstacles. The life-long friends who shared the challenges, pain, and wonder. The spectacular moments of our country laid out before me. The uplifting generosity of people over and over again. Doing the right thing in the most elementary way.

I honestly believe that the AT thru-hike brings the best out in those who do it—in a way I haven't discovered in any other life experience.

I am really a better person because of this. I wonder if this "betterness" will endure back in the world of compromise? I don't know if goodness is learned or innate. I tend to feel it is learned. I was surrounded by so much goodness growing up; particularly my parents and siblings, most particularly my brother, that I recognize goodness when it is in evidence. Goodness comes under constant threat for the rest of our lives, and compromise drains it. It is replenishable, but replenishing requires a recommitment and an effort. The AT experience, in my view, is one such effort. So the journey has certainly maximized its welcome, and I am ready for the finish. But once completed, I know now, it will be missed.

My friend, Pipe Wrench, tells me it was here where my inner journey was complete. That from here to Katahdin was a worldly pursuit. In fact, our Shakespearean of the Trail, April, calls Katahdin the "goal-infested northern terminus." She split off the AT in Vermont continuing north on the Long Trail, not feeling a need to go on to Maine. She felt she could reach her spiritual conclusion in the Northern Kingdom. Maybe they both are right, but I can't imagine stopping four-fifths through. I am sure the last fifth will create wonderful memories.

So here I go.

E-mail #39–Map Marker #64

Maine

I have returned to the Trail from home. This was the hardest return. I am ready for this to be over.

The area that I will be hiking in, the southern-most sections of Maine, was sculpted by the Ice Age. Not that long ago, barely 150 centuries, Maine was under ice. How much? Katahdin was under ice, completely. Katahdin rises over 5,000 feet; the ice was more than double that. The pressure and weight changed Maine enormously, only to change it again as oceans of water poured through its notches as the ice melted. It left a series of lakes, massive potholes, cliffs and valleys, unmatched anywhere else in the eastern portions of North America. Were I flying, I would love Maine above all the rest of the AT. In that I must hike, I have a different emotion altogether. I have to hike around the lakes and ponds, through the potholes and notches, up and down the cliffs, and over some of the nastiest mountains on the AT.

Mahoosuc Notch is called the "hardest mile on the AT." It is a valley where house-size boulders were deposited. The hiker's job is to go over, under, and around these boulders, often removing his backpack in order to crawl up or under a boulder. It is a monster, but really, it is only a mile. A thru-hiker is daunted by the long haul; that's what being a thru-hiker is all about.

Maine returns us to the cultural heart of middle America. People live simply here. Uncomplicated people. Hardworking and serious. I very much like every person I have met in Maine. The state motto, "The Way Life Should Be."

E-mail #40–Map Marker #65

Maine spins its charm.

Superstition prevented me from talking about or making plans for the finish. Now I think about it everyday. Maybe every hour. I am two sections into Maine, barely 25 miles. I summitted Baldpate, twin peaks on a clear day, and I was stunned visually. Hundreds of mountains were laid out in front of me 360 degrees around. A panorama. I never knew or expected Maine to have such beautiful vistas. I turned my phone on, and as often happens on the peaks, I had 5x5 reception. I wanted to share this beautiful moment with Dana. Didn't happen. She was out taking care of everything I have been ignoring for six months. But I am excited about her hiking with me at Katahdin.

While I was at home, friends asked me to write often for the last few days. They also wanted me to talk about how I feel, and what I think. Maybe for the last few days, I will dig a little deeper and try to unravel the reason for this quest.

Tonight, I am in Rangeley. It is a pretty little town—a lake town. This part of Maine is more than 50 percent lakes. When you consider the mountains, which are mostly parks or reserves, there is little space for development. Not much space for people. It keeps the population of Maine down, which isn't all bad.

But the lakes are busy, therefore, so is Rangeley, unlike the balance of Maine. Maine is struggling. Rumford, down the road, has lost 50 percent of its population. It is a paper town. Because of union demands, mechanization and consolidation, the workforce and employment has reduced. Everyone points their finger at others.

Politicians turn their backs on a state with only 4 electoral votes.

The reality is that little one-industry industrial towns are doomed.

Pittsburgh had the critical mass and clout to reinvent itself, and it did. Rumford is doomed.

But where I am in Rangeley is beautiful and bustling. The lakes are an economy of their own. Real estate and tourism. It works.

For me; a great IGA (grocery store), CVS (pharmacy), and an AO (Appalachian outfitter). I also sleep in a B&B for some TLC.

E-mail #41

The future of the AT

I've been told by a few people who seem to know, that the number of thru-hikers who made it to Maine this year is substantially down. The explanation is a higher than normal dropout rate. That squares with my experience. Almost none of the characters I wrote about in the early chapters ever reached Maine.

I would like to get the real numbers from the ATC, but there is a legitimate worry here. The infrastructure of the AT is fragile. The merchants, hostel owners, and outfitters who support the hikers are always close to the bone. It worries me that many may drop out, making it difficult for future thru-hikers. I know in my experience many businesses listed in my reference materials are now gone—out of business.

I hiked all day today, and saw no thru-hikers, northbound or southbound.

E-mail #42–Map Marker #66

The Rangeley boat

Mooselookmeguntic. What a name. This is the name of a lake, a big lake. It almost touches the AT in two spots. I am guessing, but it seems to be about 30 miles long. It connects to Rangeley Lake, about half that size, and then they both connect to Flagstaff Lake, much bigger than the two combined. Then on and on. This part of Maine is mostly water.

There are international canoe competitions through these lakes and world-class fishing. These lakes support Rangeley in the summer and become part of hundreds of miles of snowmobile highways in the winter. Highways leading to, and connecting to, similar highways in Canada.

Rangeley is also known for its century-old fly-fishing boats. They appear to be canoes, but they are not. They are much more stable and actually lighter per foot than a wooden canoe. But often much bigger or longer. They are made of a wood that swells when wet. So the boat is built, full of openness, and then it is taken out to the lake and sunk. The wood swells, it is dragged from the lake, bailed out, and now all the wood has swollen tight and the boat is waterproof.

After it is bailed out, it floats.

The original boats are priceless. The original boatmaker's grandson, who is 70 years old, is still a boatmaker.

One by one, he builds the Rangeley boats.

I love everything about Maine. Except the Trail.

E-mail #43

Strong, clean hands

Bob the B&B owner keeps a '55 Chevy Convertible in storage. He got it out and drove it last week. I wish he would get it out now, so I could see it.

Bob has a friend's son living here. This boy needs the warmth that Bob shines on all of us. I hope it helps.

Bob and I found ourselves in a long conversation today; I discovered his two sons aren't biological.

Turns out that, years ago, another set of friends of his were getting a divorce; they were slashing each other during the contentious process. These two little guys were caught in the middle. Their parents were smart enough to get them out of the cross-fire.

Bob took them in for a week or two. They stayed. 33 years later, they still look at him as their father.

Bob is 70. Very intelligent. He has strong, clean hands that move over the steering wheel as he shuttles me to the trailhead. He has a warm deep voice.

He worked for 30 years as the head of an Easter Seals Camp in Massachusetts. Here is a man who has done only good his entire life. Now in retirement, he runs a place where hikers and snowmobilers can rest.

When Bob dies, they should save him, freeze his body maybe, and kick Ted Williams out into an alley to thaw out.

E-mail #44–Map Marker #67

I crossed paths with Gucci and Hooch today.

I was struggling up a very difficult Moody Mountain. They were coming down. We knew we knew each other, but it took a while. Breakfast at Gatlinburg, Tennessee! Five centuries ago!

They looked fabulous. Gucci, of course, with all the latest everything. Hooch, never prettier or nicer. They moved slowly and didn't arrive at Harper's Ferry until July. I was far ahead in Connecticut by that time.

So, they flip-flopped and flew to Maine. Flip-flopping is the term for hiking a part of the thru-hike in one direction, usually north, leaving and flying to the other terminus and finishing the hike going to where you left off. They hiked to the top of Katahdin, and have started south. They would have never reached Katahdin before Baxter State Park closed for the winter, so this was a smart move.

They will finish at Harper's Ferry, my guess would be in November or December. A nine-month adventure. They were happy and still excited. They told me I looked better, not so skinny. They laughed and headed down.

I watched them go down, then I continued up.

E-mail #45–Map Marker #68

I fear the dragon.

Today, I am crossing Bemis Mountain. A dreadful PUD. There is nothing redeeming about this crappy little mountain. The Trail managers of Maine sent us to the top of it.

The locals know that the top of Bemis is a waste of effort and time. They dump the AT and go their own way. They go down something called the Valley Trail. One mile closer, and no damn PUD.

So I'm walking across the rock top of this mountain, no view, of course, and the dragon strikes. He strikes where I should have always known he would.

He does not scrape me off the Trail, he extends a claw and pierces me, stabs me in the back. The pain is immediate and excruciating. I am paralyzed. I stop and am dropped to one knee.

There didn't seem to be anything in particular that happened when the pain struck. But it is familiar.

It has happened so often. For some reason, the dragon waited 1,931 miles to do it on this trip.

I am, of course, alone. Five miles. Five incredibly difficult miles to get any help.

Finally, the pain subsides enough to let me stand. A few minutes later, all hunched over, I can take a step. Then two. Slowly, I head down Bemis-fuckin-mountain.Then walk, and I slowly head down.

Maine requires rock-scrambling, hand over hand at least every hour, and fording streams.

I have no idea what is confronting me on the Trail ahead, and my left side isn't working very well. The constant pain isn't my biggest problem. I don't want to be in a tricky place and be pierced again.

Maine requires you to hang out over open spaces too often.

After what seems to be forever, limping along, I come upon a sign, telling me I am 1.5 miles from the road where I am to meet my shuttle driver. Fortunately this was a day Bob and I planned. He is picking me up. It is now straight uphill to the road.

I did okay going down, I don't know if I can go up.

I can, and I do. I lay down next to the road, and Bob shows up about half an hour later. At first, he misses me because I am lying down. I whistle and he comes back.

Tonight I feel better. I have been lying on the floor in Bob's little kitchen. I am going to try to hike tomorrow.

The pain is one thing, but if I have an event like today, it renders me weak; my upper body seems too heavy for my back to support. The dragon did his worst. This is what I have dreaded.

E-mail #46

The pain is weird.

Preparing for today's hike, I do everything I know to support my back. I stretch out, I wear a back brace that I have been carrying. I will slack-pack today regardless of price. Bob will drop me where he picked me up yesterday and pick me up 13 miles forward. It is a dirt road known only to locals. I take Vioxx, then it is time.

The 13 miles are not terribly hard. The weather is hot but dry. Okay by me, I don't want any slippery rocks.

The pain is weird. Yesterday and last night, it was on my left side. It extended down my hip, but concentrated in the left side of the small of my back. I didn't sleep well last night.

As I hike today, the pain moves around and finally centers on my right side. But it seems to have lessened.

Five miles. Eight miles, ten miles, then it is over. The pain in my back is much better. I am relieved. Tomorrow will be a very difficult day. One of the toughest mountains to climb, Saddleback Mountain. If my back holds together tomorrow, it will be a blessing.

I celebrate as we pass through Rangeley with a Frappe (pronounced Frap). It is a very thick milkshake. If you order a milkshake, you get chocolate milk. If you want ice-cream and you want it blended, you order a Frappe extra thick.

One of the guests here at the B&B is grilling hamburgers.

Today is so much better than yesterday.

But there is no doubt—I fear the dragon.

E-mail #47

Quebec pride

Today was a very hard 15 miles over Saddleback Mountain. It is easier northbound, however, I took it southbound for an unimportant reason and regretted that decision. But a big thing still happened.

First, the dragon did not attack today. Secondly, I moved into single digits as a percentage of what's left. I am under 10 percent. I am now less than 110 miles to the beginning of the 100-Mile Wilderness. The AT's final fast ball.

In the 100-Mile Wilderness, there are no stores or stops; you must carry everything on your back the entire way. The sign at the beginning of the Wilderness says to carry 10 days worth of food. Northbounders flip a bird at this sign. No way we are going to carry that much weight.

At the Piazza Shelter, I ran into, for the second time, a French-Canadian teen hiking club. Maybe 20 teens. Out of the 20, only 3 spoke English. Very interesting that our closest neighbors' children don't speak much English. Quebec pride, I guess, that they wouldn't speak the language of their own government, or the established international business language, or the language of their closest neighbor. While I can understand Quebec pride, I cannot understand parents penalizing the children in this secular way. Very small-minded, but no one asked me.

Two days ago, I was at a different shelter when I ran into this same group.

One of their leaders came back from the water source. He said something to the group. It had a bunch of "ou" kind of puckered sounds, then ended with "sheet hole."

I agree. The water source was a sheet hole, and I'm glad he didn't let them drink from it. Even purified.

Saddleback and Ballpate are the two best views in Maine so far. The Trail is very difficult because it is so gnarly. Roots, high roots, grow all over the Trail, like a scene from a horror flick. My feet and ankles are constantly slipping and twisting. Picking up any speed is impossible. I am barely averaging 11 miles a day, and I am exhausted at day's end.

Gnarly is a Maine word for "sheety."

E-mail #48–Map Marker #70

I catch up, reading the Shelter Registers.

I keep passing milestones. Today I passed the 2,000-mile point. By the end of the day, averaging 14 miles a day, I should have 14 days to the finish. Today is the 14th of August; maybe I can finish before Labor Day. Each zero adds a day and I have gone six days since my last one. I am told I could put up some 20s further north.

And there is a bigger problem. The dragon.

Today is a hard day, but I've had many harder. It is over Spaulding Mountain and Sugarloaf Mountain, and it finishes in a Valley called Caribou.

After a break at Spaulding Mountain Shelter, I begin the second half of my day, and my back strikes, worse than before. I stop, take a second Vioxx, tighten the back brace as much as I can, and finish the day through some treacherous down hills. Amazingly, I discover that a hostel in Caratunk, the town I will enter in two days, has a massage therapist. I've had some good luck with massage helping my back in the past.

I have booked myself for a session. But to get to the session, I have to get there. No slam-dunk.

To happier things.

I hiked the entire section alone today, but not really. I came to a lean-to, which is a Yankee term for shelter, and sat down for a break.

As I was looking at the Spaulding Mountain Lean-to's register, I kept coming to old friends.

The Flying Pork Chop was here July 27. With 12 days to go, at his speed, he has reached Katahdin. He has crawled up onto the Katahdin Sawhorse on top of the mountain, raised his trekking poles in the air and had his picture taken. The traditional finish.

Maybe a loved one took the picture. Maybe it was his fiancée, maybe she walked up with him. Maybe a hiking buddy. Or maybe Porky walked up alone, had a stranger take his picture, and then he sat on a stone off by himself and wept.

I can see Porky doing that—what a great guy.

Giggles' dad is sick—very sick. She left the Trail to go home. Giggles and Highwater were out of money in Pinkham Gap. They were exhausted, having been taken off Mount Washington because of the storm, the same one that caught me on Mount Madison. They were dirty, exhausted, and so very much wanted a shower and a bunk in Joe Dodge Lodge. I felt so guilty. I had a private room. It was just a sliver of a room, not 8 feet wide, but to hikers it was a suite.

Well, to shorten the story, I sprung for a couple of bunks and a breakfast for the two of them. 42 whole dollars.

I told them it was a loan, and if I'm ever in Quebec, I expect a bunk and breakfast.

I would soon be going home for some meetings, so I really didn't think I would ever see them again. I did, however, shortly after breakfast the next day. We hugged and I said good-bye. They looked clean and fresh, ready to finish.

Now the shelter registers tell a different story. Extrapolating, they seemed to have stopped somewhere. Because of Giggles' father, finally Giggles went home.

Highwater sounded completely lost as she wrote in the registers. The two of them had been a team for 1,900 miles. Now Highwater is solo. I saw one register where she was only one day ahead of me, then with a 20, walking until midnight, and an 18, she is two days ahead. Her writing sounded better. But she should not be night hiking in these mountains, and she knows it.

Out of nowhere in the Spaulding Mountain register, she wrote, "Bearfoot, are you back there?" Really made me feel good, but sad too. Otter and Pipe Wrench are somewhere around her. They will take good care of her.

A day or so earlier, I saw Pipe Wrench's distinctive handwriting. His words were a little hard to read, his hand seemed to be shaky from exhaustion. Pipe Wrench loses too much weight. He can get down to 135, when his normal pre-hike weight is 170. I worry about him. But I could read it. It said, "Here for the night. Hard day. Welcome back Bearfoot. Pipe Wrench." The date was the exact date that I returned to the Trail. Amazing.

Others were evident. Tired, sick and tired, disgusted, but unbowed.

Absent the dragon, they will all finish, and all before me. I send ahead my love and respect. Feel me with you guys, you are all the best.

E-mail #49–Map Marker #71

A call to an old friend

I am bunking in with Pinecone tonight. Remember him? The son of *Pinetree*, my buddy in North Carolina?

Anyway, we get a phone to work, and we call Pinetree. It is great to talk to him. He had returned to hike with Pinecone through some of the sections in New England. He has a bad knee now, so it doesn't appear that he will be doing anymore hiking for a while.

But his good humor and good will came over the phone lines. He says he is coming to Katahdin to see Pinecone finish. This should be about the time I get there. Maybe I'll see him. I hope so. Having a friend there would be special to me.

I am now moving through the Bigelows, the last major mountain chain before I get to Katahdin. I will be in Caratunk next, a small hiker's town. Then Monson, the last town we pass through. There are 188 miles left. I will do 17 tomorrow. It will feel good to knock off some miles.

The dragon was busy with other things today. I am trying to sneak through the rest of Maine, hoping not to catch his attention. I spoke to Dana tonight; she is a little scared about Katahdin. But she can do it.

In the next day or so, I cross a major river, the Kennebec. Steve Langley shuttles hikers across in a canoe. Years ago, hikers forded the Kennebec, but upstream dam openings led to fatalities.

Steve has done this for 16 years. He loves being part of the AT adventure. His father was the former Governor of Maine. But he isn't a politician, just a hiker; and he has a hiker's hostel in Caratunk. I look forward to meeting him.

E-mail #50–Map Marker #72

The river, the canoe trip, and Caratunk all went without any problems. And I think the massage helped.

Steve Langley is a nice man, but he is burned out. It's good this is his last year as the canoe shuttle-ist. But I'm glad I got to meet him. He is an AT legend.

I have completed everything considered difficult but the 100-Mile Wilderness and Baxter State Park where Katahdin rests. There are 145.8 miles to its peak. Unfortunately, once summitting Katahdin, you have to come down. Meaning, another five miles. Then we work our way home.

Maine has been full of mountains, and the AT insists we summit all of them possible. Maine has reminded me of the term "false summit." We saw a ton of these in Georgia and North Carolina.

A false summit is as you go up; there is a visual reckoning that tells you that you are near the top. It has to do with tree angle, the view of the sky through the trees, and sometimes the slope of the Trail.

However, some mountains fool you. You think you have reached the top, but the trail turns left or right, and out of nowhere, there is more mountain. Lots more mountain. How could that be? A mountain is not small, you know, hard to hide. You realize you have much more climbing to do. It appeared you were peaking, and things would be a bit easier, but it is not to be. This is a false summit. You must dig in and find some reserves somewhere. Then keep on climbing. Maine's mountains are full of false summits.

Not unlike life. When things are seemingly at their hardest, they get even harder. You go on. Or you just sit down and quit.

E-mail #51–Map Marker #73

The famous Shaw's in Monson

I am in Monson staying at the famous Shaw's. Keith Shaw, all 5'4" of him, is the patriarch. At 73, he is a medical miracle. Eight bypasses—yes, I said eight. One removed lung later, his scars are twice the length of his height. I know. He showed them to me.

Pat, Keith's third wife, takes care of reservations and cooks dinner. She looks and acts permanently exhausted—and probably is. The glue that holds Shaw's together is Keith, Jr. At 22, with a Jay Leno chin, and every other tooth, Keith, Jr. is upbeat, welcoming, and makes it all work.

Keith, Jr. shuttles hikers all around this part of the state, which makes Shaw's a hikers' center.

They once were known for their meals. Breakfast is hearty, and all you can eat. But Keith, Sr. has lost his fastball behind the skillet. (Miz Jenny in Damascus now is the AT's best breakfast.) Dinner is cooked by Pat, and the meal is just as exhausted as she is. But the shuttle brings many hikers to Shaw's, just like a bus depot, so we can get a slack-pack in either before or early into the 100-Mile Wilderness.

But Keith, Jr. is more than the shuttle driver. He is the guy who makes you recommend Shaw's to next year's hikers. While Keith, Sr. and Pat are perpetuating the tradition, Keith, Jr. is the reason you are glad you are there. Without him, the Pie Lady would rule Monson.

Because Shaw's is the funnel all hikers pass through to the 100-Mile Wilderness, there is a great opportunity to see old friends.

Turkey Bacon—what a shock—is here and we catch up. How can one person be so accomplished at pissing everyone off? Tin Man, my brother-in-law's friend, shows up. Sans Ruby Slipper and Toto.

Grits, a Valdosta, Georgia, guy, also makes an appearance. *Black Hawk* and *Squaw*, a really neat couple I'm getting to know, also come through. Remember Will and his hound dog, Herbie? We were together at Mountain Moma's. They've developed a moniker. They now call themselves *Herbie and I*. Will's Trail Name is "I." It's very interesting for somebody to call him I as if it's his name. Confusing too. Herbie is the hound dog that I (me, not him) was worried about being dragged into the mountains. Back in Georgia, Herbie ran away the first day and showed up again the third. I guess he decided hanging in with Will was better than being alone in the forest. Actually, he's grown stronger, and seems to like his days better.

I've come to know another couple. *Cracker Jack* and *Midnight Sun*. I sponsored a barbeque and beer night around the corner from Shaw's and found myself talking to them. Really neat folks. Midnight is from Alaska and has great plans—but is not sure of anything. Huh? Cracker Jack has a dog named Jack, seems backwards to me.

The best news is that Giggles showed up. Her Dad, who had a very close call with the Grim Reaper, revived, and sent her back on the Trail. She and Highwater are together again. They are hiking with *Poet*. Poet is an ultra-shy fellow who comes alive with a pen in his hand. While he almost never says anything, the shelter registers are blessed with his talent. I have often wished that I started copying his poetry from the very beginning. Poet is the perfect companion for these two, they will stay together to the end. I had not seen Poet since the tornadoes near Pen-Mar.

My second day at Shaw's, Keith, Jr. asked me if I wanted to go get a beer with some friends of his at "The Camp." I said sure.

The Camp is a bear camp. It sits in something called Land Share. Land Share is massive expanses of forest owned by paper companies, but they let folks use the land much like a national forest would. It has a gatehouse, permits, campsites, and so on.

One thing they permit for is baiting and running bears.

Bear hunting.

These guys explain it to me.

Baiting.

First you have to have a bait permit. What is the bait? Two-day old doughnuts. They put thousands of old doughnuts in a pickup truck bed and drive around logging roads and dump them out in high piles. Thirty-five piles because they have 35 permits. Why? Because the hunters don't want to go up into the mountains where the bears are. So the guides bait the logging roads to bring the bears down to the hunters.

Then about two days before the hunters come, the guides let their dogs loose. The dogs all have GPS collars. Now the intwepid hunter (Elmer Fudd language) or in other words the IH, comes to the camp and starts drinking beer.

Eventually, a poor bear, addicted to Dunkin' Donuts, leaves his home and comes down to the bait. The dogs run the bear, finally, up a tree.

The GPS tells the guides that the dogs have a bear treed. Guides and IHs jump into their trucks, half beered-up, flying down logging roads. These are private roads, so there is no DUI. The GPS takes them straight to the site. Sometimes it is 100 yards or so to where the bear is treed. And the IHs get their boots muddy. This really pisses them off, and the guides apologize profusely.

Then they walk up to the tree, shine a spotlight at the terrified bear, and blast away.

Horrible.

E-mail #52–Map Marker #74

I feel Katahdin in every pore now.

I am flying. Today a 19, yesterday over White Cap 21. The day before 17. I am 45 miles from Baxter Peak atop Katahdin Mountain. A beautiful view of Katahdin is written about from White Cap Mountain. It is something I looked forward to for hundreds of miles. Today, I am pushing my way up that impossibly steep mountain; Southbounders are passing and telling me how spectacular the view is.

An hour before I reach the top, it starts to shower. By the time I crest it is raining hard, there is no visibility, and there won't be for the rest of the day.

The summit is deserted. The winds and rain rumble my rain suit. I look in Katahdin's direction—but see nothing. The northbound blazes lead down the other side of the mountain. I follow.

E-mail #53–Map Marker #75

I added a drop or two of salty water...

The next morning the sky is crystal clear, but I am down in the forest in a tunnel of trees. There will be no view of Katahdin from here. The day is crisp and cool. There are no more mountains between me and Katahdin.

Maine flattens out now for about 60 miles. Then this fabulous mountain rises, almost perpendicularly to 5,267 feet.

The Trail today is kind. Level, not too rocky or root filled. I am actually able to have a pace—to have some rhythm in my hike.

As depressed as I am about not seeing Katahdin yesterday, my spirits improve because of the beauty of this section. The trees are brilliantly green, and are sparse enough to catch water views.

The Trail wanders through some of Maine's most beautiful ponds and lakes. Crawford Pond, Cooper Pond, JoMary Lake; and then Pemadumcook Lake. About 14 miles into my day, I come upon a small wooden sign, maybe 4x6, nailed to a tree, "Katahdin View" it said with an arrow pointing towards the water. The water was approximately 75 feet to my right. Still under the canopy of trees, I walk forward. I can see mountains out past this vast lake, but I can't tell which is Katahdin.

I come out from the trees, step on the rocky shore, and I look harder at these mountains; but something makes me look left, hard left. All the air left my lungs. My jaw drops. There, completely filling the north horizon is this one, massive presence. Not part of a mountain chain, but all by itself.

Katahdin.

"There you are big fellow," I said aloud. "I've waited so long for this moment."

To get the best angle to view Katahdin, I take a few steps into the shallow water, and turn towards the old man.

I don't know how long I stand there. My poles and boots are in 4 inches of water, my elbows rest on the handles of my poles, and my chin is cupped in the palm of my hand.

How many before me must have been transfixed in this spot? Did they look at the scars running up the old man's side? The trees that gave up trying to root about halfway up?

He looks as if he grew out of the lake. Massive, magnificent.

Katahdin.

A worthy terminus.

I add a drop or two of salty water to Pemadumcook Lake.

I smile again and shake my head. Then I go about the business of photographs, and getting my wet shoes out of the water.

I am so very close. Three days, then wait a day or two for Dana, then summit. Be nice to us, old man, and please keep that dragon inside his cave. Could you do that?

E-mail #54–Map Marker #76

. . . the last morning I will break camp.

I wake up at 5:30 a.m. It is Sunday morning, August 25. I slept fine in the Rainbow Stream lean-to.

The sound of the stream running 20 feet away entices me to turn over, but I don't.

Unzipping my sleeping bag, I realize this was the last night I would sleep in it, maybe forever. It is my summer bag. It was cold last night, so I wore everything I had with me to bed, including my rain suit.

After a quick visit to the privy, I take my titanium pot to the creek and fill it with water. I do not need to purify since I will be boiling this water. I break open my ezbit stove, pulling out the legs where the pot will sit. At the bottom of the stove, I place a burn cube and light it. I cover the pot. The pot's top can also double for a skillet, although I have never used it for that. While the water comes to a boil, I pull two cocoa packets out of my food bag and a power bar. Checking the water, I start to stuff my sleeping bag into its stuff sack.

Next, I disassemble my insect tent. It is geeky looking, but it works perfectly. Assembled, it is a little dome maybe two feet tall. It covers my head and arms down to about my waist. I can read, write, sleep, and toss and turn, and it stays put; and most importantly, no bugs or mice get to me. My tarp pack was my pillow last night. I place it, my sleeping bag and my insect tent in the bottom compartment of my backpack.

I decide to boil the water a little longer than usual so I drop another cube in the stove. We are in low altitude, and for all I know there could be a cattle farm up stream.

I take my sleep pad and roll it up and place it in the main compartment of my backpack. The pad starts to unroll the minute I place it in, and it becomes the "walls" of the pack.

My feet require attention. I start putting different kinds of tape and band-aids on several spots on my feet, different types of tape for different places. But on top of all of that, I cover it with duct tape. Liner socks on top of the tape, socks on top of the liner socks, then my New Balance hiking sneakers. Finally, on top of the sneakers, ankle gaiters. Gaiters keep stuff from getting into your shoes. They keep my laces tied, and keep my laces from getting caught on something and causing me to trip. I wore my knee braces to bed last night, so I didn't forget—as I often do—to put them on, and therefore, have to undo all the shoe gear and start over. I take off all the clothes I had on when sleeping, and stuff them into their stuff sack. Even though it is still cold, I will warm up considerably when I start hiking.

I pour the hot water into my cup filled with cocoa mix, and stand next to the creek for several minutes to enjoy my hot chocolate. I fill the food bag with pots, stove, lighter and trash and drop it into my backpack. After taking a couple of pills, dropping eye drops onto my contacts, and brushing my teeth, I drop my toiletries bag on top of the food bag. Clothes stuff sack goes on top of that. I am okay for water, so I don't touch the bladder compartment of my backpack. Books go in the top zipper. Headlamp, the side zipper.

Now there are three clips to clip, check the five zippers, are they all zipped closed? I have lost stuff forgetting to zip a zipper.

Put on my back brace. Pull the backpack up and behind me in one smooth motion, slipping my arms in the shoulder straps; clip the fourth clip across my chest. Yank strong, long, and hard on the hip belt. There are six straps to adjust. Now my backpack is on.

Where things go in a backpack is a personal decision. Also, what is strapped outside. I find, however, that a new hiker will have all kinds of stuff hanging outside the pack. And an experienced hiker will have almost nothing. Generally you want your heaviest items as high as possible. Large items can only fit in the main compartment and lower compartment. A hiker wants to be able to find whatever is needed easily and in the dark. So once you pick a spot, you keep it.

I reach to pick up my breakfast off the rock I have placed it on, the Power Bar. I pick up my trekking poles. Black Hawk is hiking with me today. He tented up the hill.

"Ready, Bearfoot?" he asks, walking down the path.

"You go on, Hawk, I'll be right behind," I say.

Almost exactly six months ago, I put a pack on my back and kissed Dana and Tallulah good-bye. This morning is the last morning I will break camp, maybe the last time I put on this backpack. The last time I will use much of the equipment and apparel I have with me. I take a moment and drink in the picture around me. Try to absorb it, commit it to memory.

As best I know, this is the last morning I will wake up on the Appalachian Trail.

E-mail #55–Map Marker #77

Beer, hamburgers, and ice cream

Today is 15 miles of uneventful Maine hiking. Rooty, rocky and slow. Every Southbounder I pass shakes my hand and expresses congratulations. They look so clean and new. They are in day one or two, and I am finishing. At the lean-to last night, there were four Northbound thru-hikers, including me, and all the rest were Southbounders. We were patient with them, and answered all their stupid questions. It was so fun to be the old pro, the experienced word. They were leaving late in a thru-hike, but Southbounders didn't have to worry about Springer closing like Katahdin would soon. Many Southbounders go on through the winter down in North Carolina and Georgia.

It seems like so long ago when I walked into the Atlanta outfitter not having the slightest idea of where to start, what to buy or what question to ask. What did I need? What was it called? The whole process was so frustrating and embarrassing. But I learned and now I am an old pro.

The Trail empties out on a paved road, I turn right and, in about a mile, I cross Abol Bridge and come to the camp store. This is the first store after finishing the 100-Mile Wilderness. Beer, hamburgers, and ice cream.

Abol Bridge is really the end of the Trail in some ways even though there are 15 more miles. Those 15 are in the confines of Baxter State Park. The first 10 are very civilized. There are 10 miles from Abol Bridge to Katahdin Stream, and five to the summit. Those last five aren't so civilized. These two sections are sometimes taken in one day. But usually they are taken in two. They become ceremonial. Often family members hike the first section, letting the thru-hiker take Katahdin afterwards. Or the reverse. Therefore there are a number of family members waiting at the store.

Everyone connects. And only Black Hawk, Herbie and I, and Bearfoot were left. Herbie and I were going to camp that night and do the last 15 tomorrow. "I" of course is really named Will; he is tough, a serious outdoorsman returning home to Maine. We hadn't exchanged a hundred words the months I had known him. Will comes over and gives me a hug. "Congratulations," he says. "I'll never forget you Bearfoot." And he and his hound head to the campsite.

Black Hawk and I are going into Millinocket about 20 miles away. The taxi pulls up. So strange, out here in the wilderness, a log cabin store, a dusty logging road, and up pulls a taxi. Unceremoniously, our hike is essentially over. We throw our backpacks and poles into the trunk.

Black Hawk and his wife, Squaw, had started at Springer 10 days after me. But we never met up or got to know each other until Shaw's in Monson. I hiked with them a full day in the 100-Mile Wilderness. She completed 2,123 miles when she could not hike anymore. Very brave lady, she had gone on for 300 miles after contracting Giardia or some other lower G.I. malady. Stopping twice to visit hospitals and take zeros, she pushed on, but now she couldn't go any further and they had run out of time.

Luckily, we were all at the White House Landing Wilderness Camp, a fabulous—once secret—hideaway. It is hidden in the 100-Mile Wilderness. The owners of the lodge promise to take Squaw (Nicole) into Millinocket to a doctor the next day. She insists that Black Hawk (Steve) continue and finish. He starts to, but he catches up with me on the Trail and tells me he isn't going to finish without her. After thinking about it, he is going to meet her in Millinocket. He knew I had a taxi coming to Abol Bridge, and asked if I would take him to town. So Nicole with 2,123 (all but 45 miles) and Steve with 2,153 (all but 15 miles) are quitting the Trail this day. They had used up their time. Steve, a Coast Guard officer, had used up all of his furlough, and had to get back. Nicole had to report to a new job, she was an airline crash inspector.

They will finish some day, Black Hawk said.

E-mail #56–Map Marker #78

Exhausted and sick

I check into the motel. I am exhausted and sick.

It was three days before Dana will come. I am ahead of my schedule by two days. I made very good time the last two weeks. That ended up being a good thing. For the next two days, I sleep most of the time.

When I call people, my voice is so gravelly, they don't recognize me. Two days of medicine, vitamins, and fluids seemed to do the trick. I will get the 10 miles in Baxter State Park done on Wednesday, the 28th, and Dana will arrive that night. We will climb Katahdin together on Thursday, August 29.

E-mail #57

I crawled out of bed.

One of my sick days, I crawled out of bed to get dressed and walk over to the Rite-Aid to get some more medicine.

Outside the motel, the taxi that picked me up at Abol Bridge two days ago was waiting for a passenger. I stopped to chat with the driver.

Out came Poet. The taxi was waiting to take him to the bus stop. He is finished. He is going home. For some reason, the sight of me stopped him in his tracks. "Bearfoot!"

he said, "I'm so glad to see you." Those were the most words I had ever heard him string together. "Wasn't it beautiful up there?"

I had to explain to him that it would be a few more days before I would summit. I went over and hugged him. He had his backpack on all snapped up. It struck me as very sweet that he did.

"Here. Take that off." I helped him stow his pack in the taxi.

He told me how perfect the weather and the view was. He told me how much he, Highwater and Giggles laughed and cut up on the top. I was so happy for him that they were with him. He would have certainly been alone otherwise. We said good-bye.

Almost all of my friends, who would have finished, have finished. I will summit on the 29th about midway through the 2002 thru-hikers who complete the entire AT. The Park stays open until October 15. Some thru-hikers struggle into November. If the weather is reasonable, the ranger will let them summit. Finally, the snows stop any further Northbounders. Southbounders will be finishing at Springer in November and December. A very few, lonely Southbounders will finish in the winds and the vicious cold of Springer Mountain in January and February.

As they arrive, they will be met by a very few clean and new looking, and over-packed Northbounders. The first thru-hikers of 2003.

E-mail #58–Map Marker #78

The next to last hike, August 28th

I've been sick—poor baby—the last day and a half. I'm in a motel in Millinocket called appropriately The Katahdin Inn. Millinocket is the nearest town to Baxter State Park, the home of Mount Katahdin, the home of Baxter Peak—the terminus, and beginning point, of the Appalachian Trail. Millinocket is one of the AT's most important collecting points. The Trail and the mountain are primary to the town's economy. It has the AT Lodge, and the Appalachian Trail Restaurant. Even though it is 20 miles away, almost every thru-hiker (if not every) will pass through Millinocket. Stay in one of the motels for the start or the finish of the adventure.

The Katahdin Inn is perfectly situated. Within a block sits a McDonald's, a 24-hour convenience store, a Rite-Aid Drugstore, a grocery store, even a going-out-of business Aymes—sort of a Woolworth's, with ultra-cheap merchandise. I crash here.

I had the flu or something—sore throat, stuffy everything, the works. I went to the Rite-Aid and bought a ton of sick stuff which I ingested, but mostly I slept. I would wake up at the weirdest times, go over to the 24-hour store, buy food, a paper (any paper), lots of liquids, and go back to my room. Then I would eat and drink, watch ESPN, and go back to sleep.

Today is the 28th. Dana arrives tonight. But today, feeling better, I hike the last 10 miles to the base of Mount Katahdin; the 10-mile stretch from Abol Bridge, where Blackhawk and I were picked up a couple of days ago, to Katahdin Stream Campground.

I decide to hike it backwards, which gives me an opportunity to do a dry run going to Katahdin Stream before tomorrow. The shuttle driver doesn't care which way I go, and tomorrow it will be only Dana and me in the rental car. The shuttle driver, who has been to Katahdin Stream Campground a hundred times, can show me how to get to the Park, what gate, where to go once I enter the Park, where I leave the car, and so on. This way, Dana and I will have a hassle-free start very, very early tomorrow.

The shuttle driver gives me the tour. Then I am dropped at Katahdin Stream Campground.

I walk over to the Ranger's Station. No one is there, but inside on the screened porch are 10 or 12 backpacks. Thru-hikers do not take their packs to the top. It is a hard climb and everyone returns here, so we slack-pack.

I check the register. Out of this 12, I only know a couple of names—and those not well. All the rest were Southbounders and section-hikers. I signed in.

I walk over to the AT. It snakes through the campground. There are very pretty campsites here. Each site has a miniature AT shelter facing the stream, very cool looking, I thought. Thru-hikers in the past stayed here and reserved a campsite free. But there is now a special spot, called The Berkshires, where 12 camping sites a day are held for thru-hikers. If you are camping in Baxter Park, which I am not, you would sign up for one of these 12 at a kiosk on the AT near Abol Bridge 10 miles away.

This is a good system because if The Berkshires are full, the hiker knows in advance, and can stay at Abol Bridge Campground, or hitch into Millinocket, or go on into Baxter Park—and illegally along the way, which is what most of them do.

I run into Tin Man. He is sitting on a picnic table waiting for his wife, Ruby Slipper. She left the Trail long ago, but is going to come back to summit with Tin Man. He doesn't call himself Tin Man anymore, but I can never remember his new trail name. We have friends in common back in Georgia, and we chat a bit. He is hoping Ruby Slipper will arrive soon, or they will have to wait a day.

I say good-bye and head south to finish off this next to last section. 10 uneventful miles later, I return to Abol Bridge Campground.

I walk up to the store, there in the bed of the pickup truck are two dead bears. The nice lady who runs the store is digging into one of the bear's feet with a hunting knife. She is removing a claw; I understand they also remove a tooth. This process has something to do with identifying the bear. They strap a chain around its ankles and haul it up on a scale. 185 pounds. A yearling, they say. One year of life.

Both hunters look as if they came from a movie set. Not a spec of dust on either one of them. I ask you—where is the sport here? Where is the hunting?

The shuttle comes and I return to Millinocket and the motel to wait for Dana. Tomorrow we summit Katahdin.

E-mail #59–Map Marker #79

August 29, 2002, 4:00 a.m.

Dana and I get dressed. She looks great, just like a hiker, not like a civilian. We carry two small daypacks. We both have trekking poles. I carry the water and the candy, and Dana carries the cameras. It will be in the mid-70s at the base, and probably in the lower-50s or colder at the peak. So we both carry layers. I will start in my t-shirt and shorts.

Last night, I was reading one of my AT trail guides, and it calls the Katahdin ascent one of the five toughest sections on the entire AT. It was included among the Mahoosucs and Dragon's Tooth. I was really worried about Dana. She is a strong and strong-willed lady, but this is a place where a slip could be serious. Most accidents on Katahdin only cause injury, broken bones and the like. But there are two rocky scramble spots specifically mentioned by the Rangers that could be fatal. An area where we will traverse a boulder, rather than climb it.

Also, these cliffs are different than most. They are exposed to the total drop. Anyone with a fear of heights will struggle with both the look and feel of Katahdin. Going up will be challenge enough visually, but coming down. . .

The cliff face and the forward roll of the mountain are straight in front of you. You will look at your toes on the rock protrusions and just in front of your toes will be a chasm thousands of feet below. I am not particularly afraid of heights, but Katahdin trained me not to look away from the part of the mountain I was climbing.

The visual invasion isn't always caused by looking down. The mountain is sheer and downward, but also rounded right and left. The sense of height can also be perceived horizontally. A surge of vertigo can hit looking to your right as easily as looking down. So the mountain is physically one of the toughest and, some say, mentally THE toughest.

But after talking to many people who had been there, I was sure that Dana could do it, and she would understand much of what I had experienced in the past six months by doing so. Also, I wasn't so sure I could stop her if I wanted to.

I intended to set a slow, careful pace. I intended to stay close. I would always be down hill, and we would do this together. People have certainly died on Katahdin, but in every case I read about, they made a bad decision often related to bad weather. And mostly, they didn't respect the mountain.

I also didn't feel it would be of any help for Dana to know how concerned I was. Rather than communicate my fear, I intended to let her know that this was very serious stuff, but I was confident of her and us. And we should enjoy ourselves. This had the added benefit of being true.

We drove through the darkness to the peak. Dana only saw the silhouette of the mountain. As we reached the campground, the day was getting light. We went over and checked in with the Ranger. As best I knew, I would be the only thru-hiker to summit today. As we approached the trailhead, Tin Man and Ruby Slipper drove by. They had summitted yesterday, and they were very encouraging to Dana, for which I was thankful.

We saw a wooden sign. 4.8 miles to Baxter Peak. There was a group of Day-hikers at the sign. A woman turned on level ground and stumbled over a stone. She fell flat and cut her leg. We hadn't even started and had already witnessed our first injury.

The Trail began quite tamely, a groomed park trail. Dead easy. It wound next to Katahdin Stream for the better part of a mile. It was completely tree enclosed; there were no views. Then, as we reached Katahdin Stream Falls, it turned upward—then more up—then viciously up, as tough a grade as I had seen the entire six months. The trees started to change, they became shorter, stunted. We often came to a sheer cliff and wondered where we would go from there, but we would find a foothold and a handhold, just enough to climb. Very often, Dana took her trekking poles and threw them up ahead of herself so she could use both hands freely.

The weather was to be clear with high clouds and patchy sun. No rain. Weather is ranked by the Rangers as I, II, III or IV. "I" is considered the best weather. "IV"—no one, not even thru-hikers, are allowed to summit. "II" and "III" have their problems. Dana and I agreed that she would accompany me if we had "I" conditions. "II" and "III," she would wait at the Ranger Station, and I would summit alone. Today's conditions were rated "I."

It became fairly cool, but we were sweating from exertion and Dana took every layer off down to her hiking pants and shirt. The fleece and jacket she started with were in the daypack now.

I followed in order to be down hill and also to give boosts when I could. It became clear that Dana didn't like boosts—so I stopped that. But I did give verbal boosts from time to time with what I thought were helpful hints. She had a very good sense of trail, and picked the right way to go almost all the time. Also, while she often chose a different ascent path than I would have, it was generally because her legs were shorter, and she was new to her poles, and didn't quite trust them yet.

On average, the Trail in the trees was about a yard wide. You would think there wouldn't be many options as to where to go to climb, but that would be wrong. Climbing is a never-ending process of decisions. Where to step. What to grab. Should I grab? Rock or root? Short step or long step? Do I ever jump? (The answer to that is always no.) Moving steadily and paced slowly, we were doing fine.

The trees opened and we had our first view. "Wow!" Dana said. A great view of a near mountain named Otto. We were already higher than its peak. We thought we saw a person on a rock over there, and waved.

We were not above tree line yet, but the vegetation was getting sparse. It was still a climb not a hike. Even at our measured pace, we passed a few day-hikers. Most of the time, however, no one was near us. We reached the tree line, and soon were above it. The climb became even steeper. All rock. We were on a vertical ridge like the corner of a building. It became so steep sometimes, there were iron rungs pounded into the rock as our only hand and foot hold.

Up we went to a ridge plateau. The ridge lay down and was a fairly reasonable uphill grade for a while, but this plateau soon stopped and turned steep again. And the climb continued. It became much cooler, and we both put on our fleece vests. This last section was the hardest and the most dangerous. It slid a bit easterly, and suddenly we were hanging over Maine—thousands of feet below. A hundred yards further, we were on top. An area called Table Top; one actually hikes here rather than climbs. Katahdin has a flat top for several square miles; then a little knob that juts up called Baxter Peak. The highest point in Maine. The terminus of the Appalachian Trail. At the highest point of Baxter Peak sits a sturdy wooden sawhorse with a wooden sign that reads, "Katahdin." From where we were—there was a mile more to hike to the sawhorse. That would be it—the end.

I spotted the sawhorse from a long distance away. It drew me, and I moved forward quickly. I looked back and realized I had passed Dana and had distanced myself from her. I stopped and let her catch up.

We reached Baxter Peak together. She pushed me in front, so I would reach the actual point of the peak first. I walked up to the sawhorse and I placed my hand on its craggy surface. I removed the blue stone from my pocket, the stone I had picked up at Springer, and I placed it under the sawhorse.

It was over. 2,168 miles. Five million steps. 14 states. Over a half million vertical ascending feet. Thousands of colleagues left behind. Other friends who had or will finish. Winter, spring, summer, and fall slipped from one to the other before my eyes in some of nature's most special spots on earth.

I feel the mountains chose me and let me finish. At any time, they could shrug me off. But they didn't. I tried not to abuse their hospitality. I tried to leave no trace. I could remember countless moments that my string had run out. Someone, or something, had to step forward to clear just one step on the Trail and help me take it. Many times it was a stranger, or a voice mail from a friend. The right word of encouragement at the right time meant so much. I felt I was doing this for all of us, with all of us.

I was brutally lonely often, yet I never felt alone. I have been loved by fabulous people in my life. Past any rational explanation. I was the renegade they chose to love in spite of my selfishness, clumsiness, and recklessness. All too often one of them would say to someone I had thoughtlessly hurt, "He didn't really mean it." Thanks for that, I promise, I really didn't.

All are here with us. With Dana and me at the finish.

E-mail #60

On Baxter Peak

My emotions were subdued. A comfortable satisfaction. My eyes have filled often on the Trail, but not here.

It seemed always important to take care of the business at hand. To execute and complete the day. Each day, I would point to a tangible goal. Pointing to Katahdin when I was thousands of miles away wasn't realistic. It would seem almost fictitious. I pointed to a target I could reach at the time: Hot Springs or Damascus, or Harper's Ferry, or Great Barrington, or Bear Mountain, or The Whites. You get the point. Only recently had Katahdin been a reality. To get to Katahdin meant completing the 100-Mile Wilderness, then climbing the mountain. Intellectually, I realized what it meant, but emotionally it was one of the critical pieces of this odyssey, not the critical piece. I knew I would make it when I stood in the shallows of Lake Pemadumcook. That was when my emotions let loose.

So getting here to Katahdin was enormously satisfying. I felt a great sense of achievement. I particularly loved the fact that Dana could share the last miles with me. But I was not overwhelmed with emotion. We had fun with the picture taking. One camera broke, but we brought three.

One other thing tempered our celebration. We had to get down. Five tough miles. Tougher than the up. There were lots of spots coming up where we said or thought, "Going down this is not going to be fun." In climbing almost all injuries happen on the return.

So back to the Hunt Trail, Baxter Park's name for the AT. And we retraced the five miles. Dana was terrific—sliding on her butt often. We called this method "The Hiney-Sliding Technique," she passed the two most dangerous sections where I held my breath. We returned to the tree line. By the way, we passed Mount Otto again and we saw that "person" in the same place. We had waved to a white rock. About here,

Dana's legs gave out; so we rested often as she wobbled to the Trail's end.

The first full day I was on the Trail, I did 8 miles, and I crashed completely exhausted into Gooch Shelter at 6:30 p.m. Dana just finished 10 miles, having never truly hiked, and did it on unquestionably one of the hardest 10 miles in North America. Pretty good stuff.

There are those who yo-yo. This is a word that's used when a thru-hiker comes to Katahdin, turns around and heads back to Springer. But for most of us, the big K is our terminus. It is certainly mine. Many, sadly perhaps most, thru-hikers, cannot say what I am about to—I can't wait to go home. While the Trail has been beyond my greatest expectations, home is a better place. For me.

We went home.

— My life is in that bag —

EPILOGUE

Two months later, my feet are changing back from leather to normal. One toe, left big, is dead. No feeling in it, and the nail which has been black for months, turned a grey color and doesn't seem to be growing out. Oh well.

I am gaining weight, about half of what I had lost. I would like to stop here.

I am in touch with many of my Trail friends, almost exclusively by email. One message was tragic. It came from a couple I always liked, but never knew very well. They began the hike as *Monkey* (she) and *McGyver* (he). But McGyver obviously didn't like his Trail name and became *Bearded Monkey* along the way. They were classy hikers; buttoned-down, organized, considerate, and well respected on the Trail. I crossed paths with them early in the hike, Pre-Damascus. After the hike, they were married.

Recently, I began a dialogue with them, and here is a quote from Monkey:

"... on a very sad note, we received a call from Pete Harley's sister ... Pete passed away on the Trail ... he was in The Whites, close to the Lake of Clouds Hut (on Mount Washington) when the weather took a sudden turn ... he died from hypothermia."

Dan Allen in his book *Don't Die on the Mountain* describes the threat of hypothermia, " ... be prepared to recognize cold hands or ears as the first indication of, potentially, your death from cold. If you are shivering, you are quite cold. The time to do something about it is immediately. ... if you find yourself becoming apathetic, you are lucky to have recognized that you have sunk to level 2. There appears to be no way you could recover by yourself from the next state of hypothermia. Make decisions. Take action."

Hypothermia affects the mind more than the body. You lose your ability to reason or make decisions. Many people found dead had taken off their clothes, thinking they were too warm. Hypothermia is grievously threatening even if you have a hiking partner. Without a partner, the danger is multiplied. The thought of Pete Harley being on Mount Washington near the warm hut of the Lake of the Clouds, and only one hour from all the facilities at the summit of Mount Washington is heartbreaking.

I later heard more about Pete. He was a bit older than me, and in the clergy. If he is who I think he is, I only met him once, but we had a good conversation. A serious wilderness adventure of any sort can and does leave its mark. Pete's family will probably never feel the risk that Pete took in hiking the Trail was worth it. But they can't ask the one who matters most, Pete.

Less tragic but something I still can't get over is the gut-wrenching story of Black Hawk and Squaw. She, only 45 miles from the end, he 15. While it frustrated me that I couldn't convince him to finish, I have to admit that I admire his decision. He simply would not finish without her. Joining Squaw was an act of valor.

The evening Black Hawk quit, he and I taxied into Millinocket. After he saw Squaw, we had dinner together. He is such a solid fellow. Just the type I would want to rescue me at sea, which is what he does for a living—a Coast Guard Officer.

Squaw is my hiker hero. Sick as a dog, she pressed on for 300 miles. When I saw her last, she must have been under a hundred pounds. Very sick. If anyone could have gone on, it would have been her, but she needed to go to the hospital—no question. I found out later that her mother had driven to Millinocket to celebrate their completion. While neither her mother, nor the two of them celebrated, it was fortunate that she was there when Squaw arrived.

I can't find Black Hawk and Squaw now. I know they are in Hawaii, and Black Hawk has joined his Coast Guard Unit, but I lost the little piece of paper I had with their real names and contact information. I am not going to give up until I find them. And sometime, years later, when they go back to Maine to finish, maybe they will let me go with them.

* * * * *

I now have a promise to keep, to answer the question most asked. Why did I do this?

There are reasons—I think. Then too, I am one of John Steinbeck's "bums."

The bum part. Months after finishing, Pipe Wrench sent me *Travels with Charlie.* The first two pages jumped out of the book. It goes ...

> "When I was very young ... the urge to be someplace else was on me ... In middle age I was assured that greater age would calm my fever...Nothing has worked ... blasts of a ship's whistle still raise the hair on my neck ... once a bum, always a bum...
>
> "When the virus of restlessness begins to take possession of a wayward man, and the road away from Here seems broad and straight and sweet, the victim must first find ... a good ... reason for going ... I set this down only so that newcomers to bumdom, like (youngsters) in new-hatched skin, will not think they invented it...
>
> "We find ... that we do not take a trip; a trip takes us ... I feel better now, having said this, although only those who have experienced it will understand it."

Steinbeck was 58 when he wrote this, I turned 57 one month after completing the thru-hike. He made the non-reason part, the bum in me, easy to explain. The reason part seems much harder, but I will try.

Business, the world I came from, was a world of math. If the numbers worked, you did it. If not, you didn't.

I believed, and believe, in the numbers. Decisions by the numbers pay off. But even as a public company's chief executive officer, I was never able to completely quiet the voice of my intuition. Gut feel. Instinct. The AT adventure just seemed to be right. My instincts told me there was more to it than just my bumness, there were reasons out there, visible, but slightly out of focus. Over the months, the picture became clearer. But then again, it may have just been a Forrest Gump moment.

I wish I could give you one, crisp answer. But like most things in life, the trek addressed a combination of needs. Here, I think, were the reasons.

Physical. The clock will win, we all know that. But we do have some say in how fast the clock will tick, and how soon it will deteriorate our body. I didn't really feel bad; I just didn't feel very well. I needed to do something physical and substantial.

Simplicity. To me, the world seems to be a poorly regulated chaos. It's just too complicated. Let's consider a phone call. Do you need to get "out?" If so, do you dial 9, 8, 0, or do you already have an outside line? When you dial, do you first dial 1 or 0? Or nothing before the area code? Do you have to dial the area code? Or do you only have to dial the prefix? And now that I'm on the phone, and I have an outside line, how do I make a long distance call? Isn't it different when I use a land line rather than a cellphone? Then we can get into cellphone roaming or not, what provider you're using, on and on. To make one simple phone call uses millions of brain cells.

I think the phone companies have committed financial suicide. Instead of offering an excellent, understandable service, they tried to turn phones into a product factory, selling hundreds of products that people would seldom use, and products that make service impossible. Telephone companies went from first to worst in customer service.

But phone companies are not alone, every life act seemed to have exploded into complexity, and I hungered for a simpler life, a sabbatical from the complex. Is rebelling from complexity a sign of stupidity? I don't think so. Some of the smartest people I know live very simple lives. They refuse to give in to complexity and the gray area. My life recently had seemed to be almost all gray area. Very little black or white. On the Trail, decisions are not easy, but once decided they are irrevocable. There is little middle ground. Very little gray.

Challenge. Many start the Trail, few finish. This is not a Walk in the Woods, as Bill Bryson said so well, but possibly the most difficult challenge the common man can take in a non-military setting. The sheer difficulty was an attraction.

Cynicism. I have become a cynic, particularly relating to my trust of people. Every thru-hiker I talked to who had completed the Trail, commented on the goodness and generosity they experienced from other hikers and those people near the Trail. To many, this was the most rewarding aspect of their hike. I had lost, or was losing faith in the goodness of my fellow man. I found my circle of trust constricting, and I hated that. Mostly, I hated what it said about me. Could this hike restore my faith?

In business, those in my firm had experienced only wins, growth and rewards for years and years. The greater that reward became, the unhappier we all became. Did we feel we didn't deserve success? Were we suspicious of it? We became cynical and ruthless. Handy with rationalizations whenever we had to explain why wrong was right.

If we couldn't handle success, I had no confidence we could handle adversity. When things got tough, and they always do, I was convinced we would circle the wagons and fire inward. I was convinced this wasn't just my partners, but human nature in general. When surprised by wealth, there is a Sierra Madre effect, turning friends to enemies. The most disappointing and distressing part of all this, was that I didn't admire many of my partners and didn't much care for the guy in the mirror either.

I wanted to reverse this. I wanted to flush the snide, the flippant, and too frequently angry person out of my system. I had no idea how hiking 2,200 miles would do that, but somehow I felt it could. I wanted—craved—to feel better about myself and the people around me. I wanted to again trust my fellow man, and be the type of person who could trust and be trusted.

Solitude. I yearned for solitude. For quiet. For alone time. That's a hard concept to explain to those you love, particularly, those who have never had this need. "How could you love me, and want to be apart from me?" I could see this question in their eyes. *It's not about you,* I would think. Solitude enhances my love for others—but that's hard to explain. Dana was supportive, and that was the main thing. I don't think she understood the concept—probably because I couldn't explain it myself—but she did have confidence in the love we shared, so I could seek this solitude without creating insecurity in her. Her most endearing gift.

Adventure. The AT is a great adventure. There aren't many left. The romance injected into my DNA by my father was seduced by this adventure. The picture of a lone man on a mountaintop, scanning the horizon, seduced me. The thought of carrying on after an injury seduced me. The cynical Pat had not exercised these feelings lately, but they had not atrophied completely. When I was planning the trek, I would often come to those quiet moments when I would ask myself, "What the hell are you doing?" It was at these moments that the sense of adventure was important.

And finally, WHY NOT? Sometimes when you're not absolutely sure why you should do something, you should evaluate why you shouldn't. As I talked to people, they would invariably say they would love to do this except. . . Maybe it was a fear of heights; no way to find the time, a fear of snakes, insects and other critters; the outdoor sleeping; the level of exertion. Some said they would love to do the hike, but they couldn't handle carrying the pack. The spouse was often blamed, he/she wouldn't understand, he/she wouldn't come along. All these—and many more—are legitimate *why nots*. But none of them applied to me. So if there was no reason not to, maybe I should. So I did.

Unlike many of my hiker friends, the AT adventure did not change the trajectory of my life. But I can't say it didn't change me. My life goals are the same; however, how I get there will be done differently.

Back at home, I am readjusting to speed. Everything is done so quickly. Conversations aren't savored; they are a series of quips and punch lines. There is little substance of conversation. Substance requires patience from both the teller and the listener.

Distractions are unending. There are far too many things to choose from.

There is a roar. There is always a background roar of people and movement. If you can't hear it, you can feel it.

Sassafras is new to me, but she is just wonderful. She has many traits similar to her great aunt, Tallulah, but she is her own person. She is much more the rascal, and I love her for that. Sapelo remains the queen of all she surveys. She is a cat's cat. Sassafras and Sapelo are friends and they play together. But sometimes Sapelo jumps in my lap and looks at me. Are her eyes asking me, "Where is Tallulah?" I respect her too much not to answer. "She is on her way to Virgil's." I say and scratch her neck.

I am spending my time doing what feels substantial. I serve on boards, both for-profit and not-for-profit. I teach. I have so enjoyed reattaching to my old friends and family. And the Georgia Bulldogs have had a great season. So home is fulfilling.

But often, particularly at quiet moments, I can taste the mist on my tongue. I can smell pine, the rich soil, and the beginning smells of life. I re-live the pure joy of surprise when a long missing friend becomes visible in the valley below. I remember when my body functioned as God meant for it to, in challenging exertion and physical accomplishment.

And I will never forget, time and time again, the smile of welcome from some total stranger who made my day better, when the only motivation to do so was the goodness that prevails in the face of all the reasons it shouldn't.

But more than anything, imprinted with clarity in my memory, will be the vista of green mountain ridges, one before the other, disappearing into the blue and gray horizon.

← Stone and Sly ↓

— Pipe Wrench is
to become a
great friend —

– April, Stone, Bearfoot,
Rawhide, Gunslinger,
Sparrow, Jeff –

– Bearfoot on a
Virginia ridge –

—The Lemon
Squeezer won't
get me—

— Wanderer. Watch out for those "raacks" —

— The AT has its OWN RR Station —

— Bear Mt Park
Observatory — a
zillion steps —

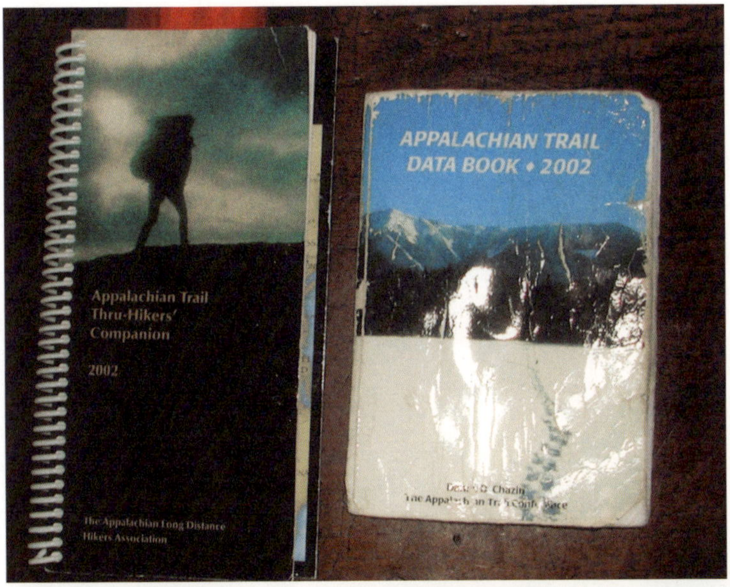

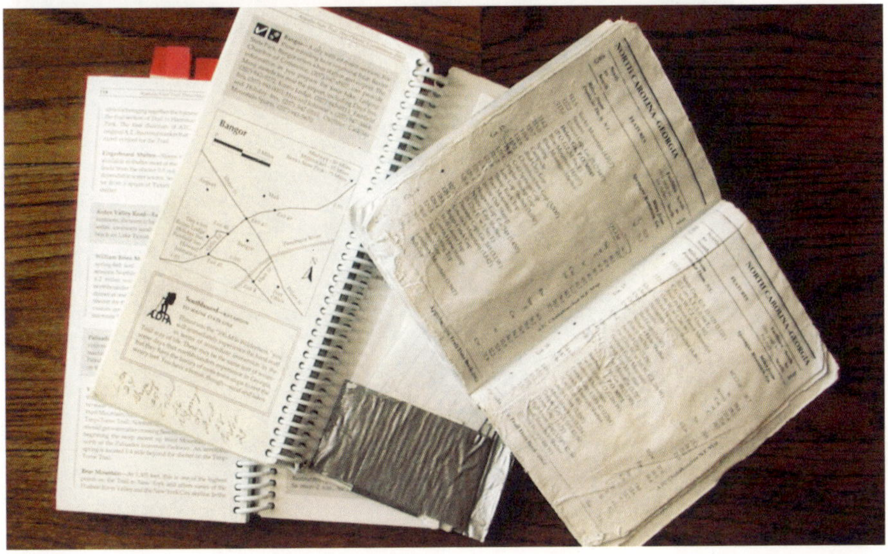

– I carried
The Data Book
and the
Thru-Hiker
Companion –

— a hang-gliders
take-off —

– April and the Cookie Lady –

– I wore out 4 pairs of shoes & held them together with Shoe-Goo and duct tape –

—Our good
friends Nancy
and David bring
Dana and meet
me on the Trail.
David hikes a
day —

— Beer & hamburgers at the Long Trail Inn
Barefoot (middle), April, Cash (always smiling), Dragonfly —

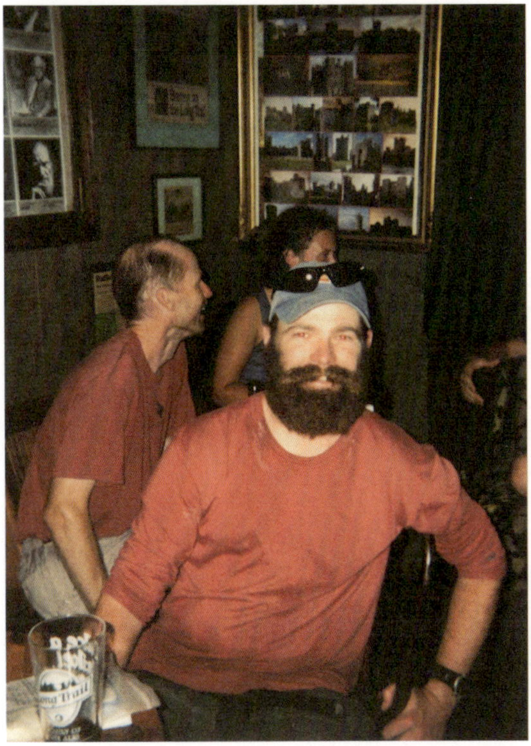

— Look at Pipe Wrench over Wizards shoulder. He is down 40 pounds. I worry about him —

— April, Cast, Dragonfly
At the Long
Trail Inn —

— Panama, under
the picture, talking
to Jitterbug —

— As brutal as
yesterday's climb
of Kinsman, today
at Lonesome Lake
is stunning —

— Bearfoot &
Birdnut

— Highwater & Giggles
at Pinkham
Notch —

—Galehead Hut
in the background.
Notice my sipping
tube below my
elbow.—

– My favorite picture
of Mt Washington –

— Playdoh coming south. Pipe wrench heading north —

— Pipe Wrench & Scout —

—Black Hawk & Squaw, a very sick Squaw—

—At each end of the "100 mile Wilderness," there is a sign—

— It's almost over —

- I finally see
Katahdin —

—Like most of
the AT, the
Trail isn't a hike,
but a climb.
Dana on Katahdin—

– Dana takes the picture, I take the traditional pose. I think… often lonely, never alone! —

What does the Trail
look like, everyone
asks

Winter - I begin

winter growth

— Walking the boards — the marshes of Virginia —

– The earliest hint
of spring –

— over fences —

— over Interstate highways —

— over rocks —

– rocks and more rocks

– The full bloom of summer –

– The boards of New Jersey –

– Massachusetts –

— Connecticut —

— Above the tree line —
— Moosilauke —

— I enter the Whites —
— The double blaze means
the AT turns —

— Cairns are blazed —
notice them on
the horizon

— See the AT climb
the mountains —

—The mountains of
Maine
Split wood boards
to prevent mountain
top erosion
The gnarly trails
of Maine —